The
Hamster

An Owner's Guide To

A HAPPY HEALTHY PET

Howell Book House

Howell Book House
A Simon & Schuster Macmillan Company
1633 Broadway
New York, NY 10019

Library of Congress Cataloging-in-Publication Data
Sikora Siino, Betsy.
The hamster: an owner's guide to a happy, healthy pet /Betsy Sikora Siino
p. cm.

ISBN: 0-87605-528-5 (hardcover)
1. I. Hamsters as Pets.   II. Title.   III. Series.
SF459.H3S53   1997
636.9'356—dc21   97-3459
                      CIP
Manufactured in the United States of America
10 9 8 7 6 5 4 3

Series Director: Ariel Cannon
Series Assistant Director: Jennifer Liberts
Book Design: Michele Laseau
Cover Design: Iris Jeromnimon
Illustration: Casey Price, Bryan Towse
Photography:
   Cover: Renee Stockdale
Joan Balzarini: 2–3, 16, 33, 74, 84, 87, 91, 101, 105, 107, 112
Trenna Gordon: 53
Cheryl Primeau: 6, 29, 30, 42, 72, 102, 116
Betsy Sikora Siino: 43, 44, 50
Renee Stockdale: 5, 8, 9, 10, 11, 13, 18, 19, 20, 21, 23, 24, 26, 28, 31, 35, 37, 38, 40–41,
45, 47, 49, 52, 54, 55, 56, 57, 59, 62, 63, 64, 65, 69, 73, 76, 77, 79, 80, 81, 88, 90, 92,
96–97, 98, 99, 103, 106, 111, 113, 114, 115, 118, 119, 124
B. Everett Webb: 32
Production Team: John Carroll, Kathleen Caulfield, David Faust, Stephanie Mohler,
   Heather Pope, Linda Quigley, Teresa Sheehan, Chris Van Camp

Contents

Welcome

to the

World

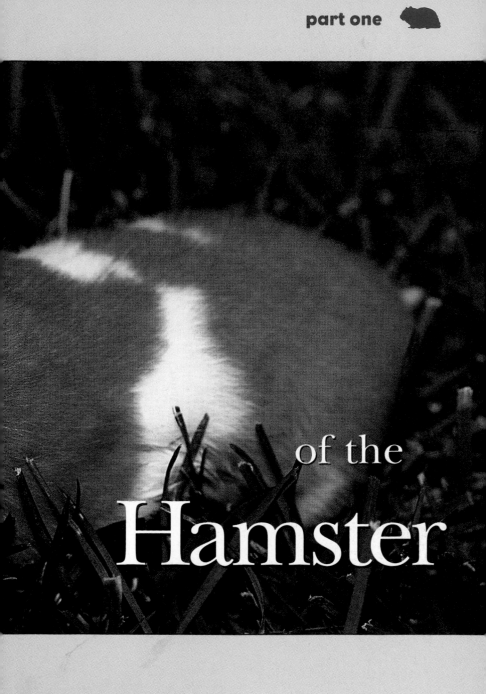

of the

Hamster

External Features of the Hamster

Eyes

Nose

Cheek Pouches

Paws

Ears

Scruff

Back

chapter 1

What
Is a
Hamster?

The hamster is a member of the rodent order of mammals in the vast sea of species that comprise the animal kingdom. The rodent order is, in fact, the largest of all mammalian orders. Approximately 40 percent of all mammal species are rodents, and almost all of those species are quite large in number.

While rodents tend to be stereotypically regarded as pests in the eyes of humans (particularly rodents of the rat and mice varieties), theirs is an amazing group of animals found all over the globe in all geographical regions and climates. Humans have access to a great deal of information about the various species of rodents, because where there are humans, there are probably rodents close by.

5

Rodents tend to live in close proximity to humans—a testament to rodent adaptability. As human populations have spread through the ages, they have invariably overtaken lands that were originally occupied by nonhuman animal species. Some species have survived the encroachment while a great many others have not.

Rodents are associated with gnawing; hence their name in Latin, *rodere,* which means to gnaw. They are able to gnaw so well because of their characteristic teeth that are designed for this jaw movement—one pair of upper and one pair of lower incisor teeth. Rodents are the most numerous of all mammals—50 percent of all mammals can be found in the order *Rodentia.*

Due to the great adaptability of hamsters, they are able to successfully coexist with humans.

Unfortunately, they are known for carrying disease and parasites and are associated with spreading (due to the fleas they carried) the Black Plague throughout Europe. To this day, the possibility of a rodent invading our food supply, home and/or workplace has caused concern for humans. If the telltale sign of a gnawed cardboard box is seen, many of us panic and start setting traps. Usually all that needs to be done to control their presence, however, is to store food correctly in secure, airtight containers.

Rodents have been domesticated for many thousands of years. It is interesting to note that if it weren't for wild rodents, we might not have the domesticated cat. Cats were called upon to control the rodent population and thus became tame and were considered part of the household. Our paths will always cross with rodents because they are attracted to our food.

Rodents and Humans

Imagine a vast forest, home for centuries to a complex, interconnected ecosystem of thousands of birds, mammals, insects and plants. Now imagine that forest is razed for cattle grazing or stripped for building identical tract homes. Just where do those resident animals go?

Those species that cannot adapt to human encroachment into their habitats are doomed either to displacement because of the loss of their food supplies and living space, or to outright destruction. This latter fate has typically resulted from intentionally destructive acts on the part of humans. Most predator species, for example, have been targeted for destruction by interloping humans, predators themselves, who have historically viewed their nonhuman counterparts on the food chain as competition.

To their credit, rodents for the most part, even those targeted just as vigorously for destruction, have not suffered the same sad fate as the predators. In fact, they have generally emerged survivors of human activity.

The names of only a few of the planet's hundreds of rodent species appear on the various lists that track the threatened and endangered species of the world. In light of the condition of most animal populations today, that is truly amazing. While individuals who do not care to coexist with mice, rats and their brethren may not be impressed by this fact, even they must admire how nature has enabled these rodent survivors to persist so efficiently.

SURVIVAL TECHNIQUES

Because most are of relatively small size, rodents may often reside somewhat unobtrusively in the midst of human domiciles, often living right under human noses for weeks or even months before a telltale chewed corner of a sack of flour or birdseed alerts their two-legged hosts to their presence.

Rodents leave signs around the house, such as chewed magazines, that let you know they're sharing your space.

Diet has also played a key role in rodent survival. Their physiological makeup enables most rodents to thrive on a variety of foodstuffs, thus ensuring that even when their favored or traditional dietary items disappear, there are always alternatives available. Most rodents can survive on a veritable smorgasbord of options, including vegetarian fare or foods of animal origin including insects and worms.

In terms of physical similarities, most rodent species are relatively small and compact. They use their delicate little "hands" to carry out a variety of functions, including collecting and manipulating food and grooming. Some rodents, such as the hamster, are graced with ample cheek pouches, in which they can store large amounts of food to hide away for a time when food is not so plentiful—a rainy day, if you will.

Physical Characteristics

THE TEETH

On a more scientific plane, we can tell a rodent, any rodent, by its teeth. The name rodent, in fact, is derived from the Latin word *rodere,* which means "to gnaw." While the various rodent species are differentiated by variations in color, size, coat type, behavior, sleeping habits, social structure and dietary preferences, all share a common characteristic in their front teeth (incisors).

The rodent incisors are marvels of engineering that continue to grow throughout the individual rodent's life. The jaw is structured to ensure that the rodent can constantly gnaw in order to keep its chisel-like incisors filed. This gnawing also allows those incisors to contact the lower set of teeth at just the right angle to finish the job. If the incisors are not properly filed—which will happen in the unfortunate rodent with a mis-aligned jaw—the animal will starve to death and suffer a great deal of pain in the meantime, as his teeth continue to grow and pierce various regions of his mouth and face.

Lettuce is one snack that hamsters might store in their cheek pouches.

HIP GLANDS

Another characteristic that hamsters have is two large glands on each side of their body, close to the position of their hips. Males have larger glands than female hamsters. The glands secrete a substance that is oily and acts as a territory marker. Their fur usually hides the glands, but sometimes a wet spot or matted fur will indicate the location on the hamster's body.

9

Some hamsters may rub themselves against the sides of their cage, imitating instinctual territorial behavior. Hamsters in the wild rub themselves against the walls of their burrows to mark their presence. Hamsters have a mild musk scent that can be detected at times when their glands are actively secreting. Since their eyesight is not strong, hamsters rely upon these scent markings to discern their territory from other hamsters.

RODENT REPRODUCTION

Due to the species' penchant for dwelling underground, hamsters only recently became part of the pet world.

To further ensure that their species survive through eternity, especially when confronted daily by successful predator species that range from foxes to bears to humans, rodents are phenomenally quick breeders. Most species reach sexual maturity within a few weeks after birth, and, if left to their own devices, rodents begin reproducing right away. As though driven internally to pass on their genetic blueprints to future generations, rodents typically produce large litters and often find themselves caring for two or three generations just weeks apart in age.

The Evolution of Hamsters

While a great deal is known and understood about the whys and wherefores of rodents, our pet hamster species have remained somewhat elusive members of that family tree because of their wild ancestors' solitary, secretive lifestyles. As is true of all rodent pets, the hamster's true beginnings are found in the wild, yet because of his tendency to burrow and spend a great deal of time underground, he was able to shield himself from prying humans for thousands of years. Consequently, the hamster is a relative newcomer to the roster of known animal species in general and pets in particular.

The classic golden, or Syrian, hamster, is the native desert rodent that evolved into several different known species of hamsters—twenty-four, to be exact—and only a few of these are kept as pets. Hamsters in general were traditionally found in a variety of regions, from mountains, to deserts, to agricultural fields. As a member of the adaptable rodent family, the hamster has been ever-nimble in his ability to deal with the elements, resulting in the evolution of a large and impressive band of hamster species.

A classic golden hamster is usually about 4 to 6 inches long.

Within the rodent order, there are several suborders, the hamster being a member of the suborder *Myomorpha,* the mouselike rodents. This includes the various hamster species, ranging in size from the tiny dwarfs that measure only 2 to 4 inches in length, to the fascinating common hamster, the granddaddy of the family, that may reach lengths of up to 8 to 11 inches, to the ever-popular golden hamster that sits somewhere between the two in size.

Types of Hamsters

As we have seen, hamsters come in all sizes, colors and geographical preferences, yet only a few species have had much long-term experience with humans. Before one simply lumps all hamsters under a single word and assumes that all are identical in behavior and lifestyle, it is wise to take a look into the world of these animals and see what differences exist between the various limbs of the hamster family tree.

WILD HAMSTERS

There is one wild type of hamster that has had quite a bit of experience with humans—most of it negative. This would be the largest member of the family, the common hamster, the only hamster that is today seen readily in the wild, although, unfortunately, not quite as readily as he once was.

WHAT IS A HAMSTER?

A hamster is part of the rodent order of mammals and is scientifically known as a member of the suborder *Myomorpha*, the mouse-like rodents. Hamsters, with their fur-covered bodies, are warm-blooded and bear live young. They reach sexual maturity within weeks after birth and are avid reproducers. Hamsters can range in length from 2 to 4 inches up to 8 to 11 inches.

A striking animal with an almost raccoonlike coat of black and brown, and quite large for an animal that goes by the hamster name, the common hamster was once abundant throughout Russia and Central Europe, but the animal's preference for a vegetarian diet would prove to be his population's undoing.

Naturally drawn to the crops cultivated on his home turf's farmlands, the common hamster was targeted, as so many rodents are, as an agricultural nemesis, his eradication proclaimed a grand mission by local farmers. The result has been a severe decline in the numbers of common hamsters in their native territory. Although common hamsters are not as plentiful in the wild as they once were, their numbers remain healthy enough to keep the animal off the endangered species list. Humankind discovered long ago that decimating rodent populations to such a level is nearly impossible.

Today there is talk of recruiting the common hamster into the ranks of the pet hamster species, where he would join the golden and the dwarf. To date, that seems highly unlikely given the common hamster's somewhat irritable and classically wild temperament when forced into captivity. Nevertheless, he remains an object of fascination to pet hamster enthusiasts, from whom he can't help but command a great deal of attention. Though he is not a classic pet species, the common hamster embodies the typical hamster characteristics to which hamster owners have become accustomed—plus, as an added bonus, a talent for swimming. All of this is found in a package much larger than we find in domestic household hamsters.

This member of the hamster family is commonly known as a Miniature Siberian hamster.

The wild species that are not typically kept as pets also include various hamsters that reside in areas as diverse as Africa, Asia and Europe. Some of these animals even have tails (the lack of a long, hairless tail is one characteristic that has made the hamster such a popular pet). These include Chinese hamsters, native not only to China, but to Europe and Russia, as well; mouselike hamsters, which call the Middle East home; and white-tailed hamsters, native to South Africa and commonly referred to as the white-tailed rat. Like their cousin, the common hamster, these species do not possess the temperament or the physical adaptability to thrive in a captive environment with humans.

THE DWARFS

The opposite may be said about the dwarf hamster, the newest arrival on the pet hamster scene. A relative newcomer to captivity, the dwarf thus far seems to be taking to life among humans quite well, and at the same time earning quite a positive reputation as a family pet.

While several dwarf species exist, the most common pet dwarf is the Russian, or Siberian, dwarf. A beautiful little creature, typically identified by his small size, delicate feet, soft coat, compact ball-like physique and the dark dorsal stripe running down his back, this animal is enjoying an ever-increasing following among those driven to live with hamsters.

While some keepers claim dwarfs are more prone than goldens to bite the hands that feed them, others find that their pet dwarfs tend to be more sociable with each other than the more solitary-minded golden hamsters. This latter camp goes on to state that dwarf hamsters can be quite docile and friendly with the humans in their lives. But such endorsements must be tempered with the warning that hamster congeniality of any species usually has more to do with an individual hamster than with the species at large—rooted in positive experiences with humans and other hamsters, and positive associations forged from being handled gently and socialized carefully from a young age.

THE CHINESE DWARF HAMSTER

This dwarf hamster looks a little like a mouse. He has two color variations: brown with a white stripe down the back and a white stomach, and white with brown patches. The Chinese hamster does not have dense hair or a stubby tail like the Syrian hamster, but his feet look the same. His body type tends to be long and thin. The personality of the Chinese hamster seems to depend largely on how he is tamed as a baby. Some Chinese hamsters are reported to be quite friendly and others tend to be difficult to handle, so it is essential that you look for breeders who hand tame their babies.

DWARF RUSSIAN HAMSTERS

There are two different species of the Dwarf Russian hamster: Campbell's Russian and Winter White Russian. Both of these hamsters have fur on their feet and short tails. The Winter White Russian hamster is the smaller of the two and has an unpointed face. They are called "winter white" because if kept in a cool environment they can turn pure white. Otherwise they are gray. This hamster is known to be amiable and easy to hand tame. The Campbell's Russian hamster is quite round and fuzzy with plentiful fur on his tail and feet. This type of hamster has many color variations including brown, albino (with red eyes), banded and dominant spot (several mottled colors), as well as cinnamon (orange fur and red eyes). The Campbell's Russian has a sleek, shiny coat similar to a satin-coated Syrian hamster.

THE CLASSIC GOLDEN

While dwarf hamsters are becoming increasingly popular additions to the pet hamster scene, the most well-known of all the hamster species, the one most commonly kept as a household pet, is the golden, or Syrian, hamster.

When stories are shared of hamsters who met untimely ends, made great escapes or in some way managed to survive loose in a home populated by ten hungry cats, you can bet the golden hamster is the star of those tales. You can also bet that when someone speaks lovingly of a hamster, an animal with whom he

---

CLASSIC HAMSTER FACTS

Classic golden hamsters are usually about 6–8 inches long and weigh 3–5 ounces. They are color blind and see their surroundings in black and white. Hamsters are most active in the darker hours, between 7 and 11 pm.

---

or she has bonded and learned to appreciate as a unique individual, that, too, is probably a golden.

As his name suggests, the classic golden hamster is gold in color: typically gold on his back with white on his underside (traits perhaps designed to camouflage the animal in his desert homeland), with large dark eyes to help the animal navigate the terrain during his nocturnal forays. But in light of the popularity of this attractive pocket pet, human tampering to alter what nature has made has resulted in vast differences of appearances within the species—and some confusion as to what constitutes a species.

This classic golden hamster, also known as a Syrian hamster, is one of the most popular types of household pets.

Technically, there is only one species of pet golden, which, thanks to careful breeding practices, now boasts a number of varieties. Colors abound, from cinnamon to cream to white to black to silver and beyond, yet purists believe that the original golden remains the most genetically healthy. Patterns abound, as well, evident in the spots and patches exhibited by so many contemporary hamsters, but one would never find such patterns on hamsters in the wild.

Also absent in the wild are longhaired hamsters or those with short, soft, velvety hair. Yet pet hamsters boasting these characteristics do exist in captivity today, thanks to breeding practices that encourage the long hair of the so-called teddy bear hamster, and the velvety texture of the satin, both of which have become quite popular pets. It is amazing to think that this dynasty began just a few short decades ago with a barrel-shaped little animal with golden fur, residing in a maze of underground tunnels in the desert.

chapter 2

Hamsters as **Pets**

A Revolutionary Discovery

The hamster has come a long way from her existence as a golden shorthaired rodent in the wild to a popular pet that may sport any variation of coat type or color and reside in domestic homes—many of those with children.

The hamster's story began in 1829 when she was discovered near the Syrian city of Aleppo by British zoologist George Waterhouse. He called this little rodent *Cricetus auratus* or golden hamster. She went on to enjoy a brief period of popularity as a pet, primarily in England. But despite their prolific breeding habits, the novelty of owning these small, unique, tailless rodents wore off and so did the existence of hamsters in captivity.

Yet the hamster would not remain unknown forever. In 1930 a zoologist named Professor I. Aharoni, from Hebrew University in Jerusalem, found a female hamster and her litter of twelve while conducting research in the Syrian desert. He had intentionally sought these animals, inspired by historical accounts he had read that described quiet, docile animals known as Syrian mice and thought to have been kept as pets by the ancient Assyrians. When the zoologist discovered the little hamster family huddled in an underground burrow in the desert, he assumed that these were the so-called mice about which he had read.

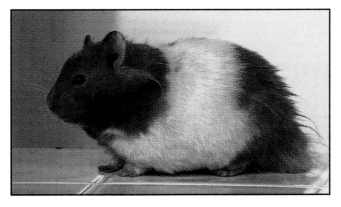

The fact that hamsters do not have a tail contributed to their wide appeal as household pets after they were introduced in the 1930s.

Most of the hamsters died when Professor Aharoni attempted to bring the mother and her young back to Jerusalem, so he was left with just two females and a male. It was believed for many years that the Syrian hamster was first discovered by Professor Aharoni but, in actuality, the Syrian hamster existed in the wild before and after the time we initially thought. It is true, however, that Syrian hamsters today have the professor's original three hamsters as their common ancestors.

While finding a family of rodents out in a desert would not at first seem to be earth-shattering, this particular discovery came as quite a surprise to those who knew rodents. Most of the few who had ever heard of the elusive hamster had assumed that the hamster species, given the animals' lack of visibility in the last one hundred years or so, was extinct, both in the wild and in captivity. But the hamster had remained unseen, not because of a decline in her population (extinction is, for all practical purposes, a foreign concept to rodents), but because her secret, solitary nature and nocturnal habits had made it so. Now, however, the secret was out, and the hamster would never again live within the shelter of obscurity.

A hamster's resourceful nature enables her to make a nest out of any available material.

The newly discovered hamster family was subsequently transported to Jerusalem. But, sadly, because so little was known about their care at the time, only three of them survived. A successful breeding program was launched with those remaining survivors, however, and today, thanks to that legendary reproductive potency for which rodents are known, each and every contemporary pet hamster is thought to be the direct offspring of those surviving three hamsters.

While their numbers began to grow and they naturally charmed the fortunate individuals who got to know them, those early hamsters and their progeny did not immediately take the pet world by storm. The species took a slight detour before that occurred.

THE ROAD TO DOMESTICITY

Once in the care of humans, hamsters were first enlisted as laboratory animals, an unpleasant fate to be sure, but one that led to an increase in the understanding of keeping the animals healthy in captivity. This information would later prove vital to the success of keeping hamsters as pets.

Today, hamsters continue to be used as lab animals, although the numbers of hamsters used for this purpose have declined substantially in the last twenty years or so. The contemporary efforts to improve experimental procedures and to reduce the number of animals used for those purposes are known as the 3Rs: reduction, replacement and refinement.

From the sterile halls of the laboratory environment, the hamster's reputation as a quiet, gentle animal (attributes that made her a desirable laboratory animal in the first place) spread. Hardly a surprise to those who had come to know her, the hamster soon found herself being targeted for a far more positive fate: that of a family pet.

The hamster proved to be a natural at this calling, of course, and has remained and blossomed within that friendly niche ever since. This great popularity is significant, considering that the hamster was officially discovered and enlisted into a partnership with humans only a few decades ago. That the hamster has become such a common household name as a pet species both in homes and in schoolrooms in such a relatively short period of time is a testament to her charm and to her decidedly ideal pet characteristics.

Clean, quiet, cute, odorless: What more could a pet owner ask for?

HAMSTER-FRIENDLY TIMES

The 1990s have proven to be an especially hamster-friendly decade as far as numbers go. As more and more people move to urban and suburban environments where pets may not be welcome, many individuals still hanker to live with animals. The hamster proves to be a natural in meeting that need. Her small size, cleanliness and ease of care mean that she can thrive in a tiny, metropolitan studio apartment with a "no pets" policy just as easily as she can in a large, suburban multi-bedroom home that hosts a variety of pets. And, according to veteran hamster caretakers, she fills the pet bill quite nicely. The hamster has been repeatedly named a popular household pet because she provides her own warm brand of companionship.

WHY A HAMSTER?

In a survey conducted by the American Pet Products Manufacturers Association, the hamster has consistently been voted the most popular small pet of the 1990s. Most people who have cast their votes for the hamster feel that they are fun to watch, and they are good, educational pets for children.

You don't hear much about hamsters in the media. They don't incite much controversy or inspire much heated debate. They don't, fortunately for them, sport rich pelts of fur like those that have made their cousin the chinchilla so legendary. They haven't become public enemy number one by entering human homes without an invitation, like the mouse. Very few associations exist for the promotion and protection of these small creatures, and there are far fewer fictionalized hamster characters than there are, say, mice and rabbits, yet their numbers are solid. The quiet popularity of the hamster as a resident in human households indicates that, within American homes, there are thousands of well-loved hamsters living peacefully and quietly, converting one person, one family, at a time to the joy that is hamster keeping.

Hamster Character

It is viewed as comedic when a hamster is cast as a mean and vicious villain in a child's horror story, or when, as occurs in the immortal comic strip "Calvin &

Hobbes," a precocious six-year-old pleads with his harried dad to read him his favorite book, one with a protagonist that just happens to be a hamster, for the umpteen hundredth time.

A hamster? What could be so interesting, so captivating about a hamster? The very existence of such questions is precisely where the humor lies. Hamster enthusiasts know that there is plenty to be interested in and captivated by this humble, unassuming animal, and that her role as clever villain and fascinating children's hero is not only pleasantly unexpected, but downright deserved. Get to know the hamster, and you will discover a quite fascinating creature that has mastered the superheroic habits of a small animal forced to survive in treacherous wild environs—an animal that is equally adept at adapting those characteristics to life in captivity.

As with all animals that have come to occupy a domestic niche, the hamster's physical and behavioral characteristics have been molded through the ages by her native home, the desert. Understand the link between the hamster's home territory and the appearance, behavior and character of the contemporary pet hamster within your home, and you will be better equipped to enjoy your pet. You will also be better prepared to offer her the optimum care required to keep a hamster spry and healthy until the ripe old age of two or three.

Hamsters make a fascinating first pet for children.

NATIVE TERRITORY

In the golden hamster's ancient homeland, the daytime temperatures were generally warm, the night temperatures cool; food was intermittently scarce and abundant; and there was little vegetation and landscaping to safely conceal a tiny rodent from pred-ators. Now envision a quiet, gentle animal—the hamster—in the midst of such a scene, and evaluate how the characteristics of her native territory relate to the hamster's evolution.

From a physical perspective, here is a small rodent whose large expressive eyes offer the first clue to how this animal would operate in the wild. A nocturnal

This hamster with stuffed cheeks is enjoying a nap after her meal.

creature requires large eyes to see effectively in the dark-ness. In the wild, she spends most of her waking hours under the cover of night, waiting until the atmosphere cools to seek her dinner. The hamster's prominent ears also have a story to tell. They are positioned high on the animal's head so the hamster might best take advantage of her acute sense of hearing, especially when faced with the challenge of detecting the presence of an approaching predator—or the voice of a trusted owner.

The ample cheek pouches are another survival func-tion of the hamster. The hamster can stuff her pouches with almost half her body weight in food, which may then be hidden in private caches for another day when food is not so plentiful (a habit pet hamsters may prac-tice in captivity, as well). This would certainly explain why this animal's name is derived from the German word *hamstern*, meaning "to hoard."

As far as hamster behavior is concerned, not much is known about the hamster's life in the wild, and appar-ently that is precisely how the hamster has intended it to be. The golden hamster remained unknown to the public at large for so long (and her natural wild existence still remains somewhat of an enigma) because of her rather mysterious lifestyle.

NATURAL BURROWERS

This is a lifestyle that took place primarily underground. A consummate burrower, the wild hamster spent a great deal of her time beneath the surface of the earth, hiding in the cool catacombs of tunnels, safe from the harsh rays of the sun, the extreme temperatures, and the teeth and claws of rodent-hungry predators. She would emerge from her safe, cool sanctuary when the sun set to scavenge for her dinner.

Food was scarce in the hamster's native territory, a condition that subsequently served to mold the hamster into an animal that requires a great deal of exercise. In the wild, she was forced to travel vast distances to find sustenance. Joke as we might about hamsters running aimlessly on their exercise wheels—miles and miles in a single day—the hamster is driven by instinct to a life of activity.

> **FROM DRY BEGINNINGS**
>
> Did you know that your fuzzy pet—queen of her habitrail—once roamed the desert? The hamster has evolved from survival in a hostile desert environment, known for extreme temperatures, a lack of shelter and a periodic scarcity of food.

Hamster owners need to understand that their pets will live longer and more contentedly if they are provided with appropriate and variegated opportunities to play and interact with people. This means making far more of an effort than simply supplying the animal with twenty-four hour access to an exercise wheel, to which the hamster can become addicted, not to mention exhausted and dehydrated.

A SOLITARY PET

The conditions of the hamster's native land, a barren landscape combined with a scarcity of food, were not conducive to sustaining large colonies of hamsters. The animals thus evolved into solitary creatures that fended for themselves. They typically came together only to mate, the female then taking on the

This sweet-natured hamster is a direct result of her attentive owner who spends time socializing and caring for her pet.

responsibility of raising her young on her own. Assuming incorrectly that a single hamster is a lonely hamster, many owners ignore the natural solitary nature of these animals, and insist on housing them together, usually with dire, and quite violent, results.

Hamster personality is also often misunderstood. Although hamsters usually prefer the company of humans to that of their own kind, they are frequently labeled mean and ornery. In most instances, the hamster that lives up to those labels is simply a hamster that has been mistreated or was never socialized to human handling. The well-bred, well-socialized hamster that is properly housed, entertained and cared for should be a gentle, sweet-natured animal that comes to know and trust her owner and to enjoy the time they spend together. Indeed the bond that can form between a hamster and a human can be surprisingly sound and touching.

The hamster, though the ideal pocket pet for the right owner, must not simply be locked in a cage and ignored. She is a solitary creature, but thrives on human care to help her adjust to life in captivity. Cleanliness, play, a healthy diet, a stress-free environment and regular human interaction are the ingredients vital to the health and well-being of this animal that boasts a long and prestigious record of survival.

Look at your hamster in light of her existence as a wild creature and you will find the best of both worlds living within your home: a delightful, gentle, entertaining pet and a creature of the wilderness all wrapped up in a single, rather adorable, package. What an honor to share your home with so distinctive a character.

chapter 3

Choosing
and **Preparing** for
Your **Hamster**

Who doesn't love a hamster? Even if someone isn't crazy about rodents because of an experience with mice or rats that invaded the kitchen, most people can't help but notice the sweet, big-eyed mug of the hamster and smile.

The hamster's charm creeps up subtly. You admire his compact, barrel-like physique, his wide muzzle accentuated by a treat hidden within his cheeks and his bright eyes and rather large nose. These characteristics comprise a portrait of a pet that resembles a tiny stuffed toy or living miniature teddy bear. Heeding your first impression, you regard the hamster as a quiet, benign, unobtrusive little creature, until suddenly you recognize something so lovable about this little rodent that you simply must spend the rest of your life basking in that charm.

Wanted: Responsible Owner

Fine examples of happy, healthy hamsters are invariably rooted with the responsible owner. This is a person who takes the time—before bringing a new pet home—to learn about the housing, diet, exercise and social interaction the pet will require if he is to live a long and healthy life. Whether one is keeping a dog or a tiny dwarf hamster as a pet, an animal deserves optimum living conditions, regular attention as well as veterinary care.

With adult supervision, kids can provide a responsible and loving home for a hamster.

The hamster owner should know the basics of hamster care and be willing to make the time and effort to do it right. The owner needs to understand the hamster's need for cleanliness and take care to keep his habitat sanitary. The hamster's bedding should be changed regularly, his food fresh and well-balanced and his access to clean, clear water constant. His owner should respect the hamster's nocturnal habits and reserve playtimes for later hours of the day—afternoon and evening—when he is most amenable to activity.

A responsible owner can be an adult or a child (many a child has actually proven to be the superior caretaker in this endeavor). A hamster is a fine pet choice for children, although his care must never be relegated exclusively to a child. While caring for a hamster presents a child with the opportunity to learn the importance of providing a pet with food, water, attention and a clean environment, this must be done with adult supervision should the child lose interest or inclination.

It's important to make your hamster feel like part of the family.

The greatest part of being a responsible owner is the commitment made to the hamster. The individual should be dedicated to providing the hamster with all the necessary amenities, avoiding unintentional breeding and spending time every day with his or her pet. In return the owner will learn how attached people can become to these wee creatures, and what a delightful relationship can exist between what was once a solitary desert dweller and the lucky person who takes him in. This often comes as a surprise to first-time owners who find themselves hooked for life after that first experience of living in harmony with a hamster.

Where to Purchase Your New Pet

Once you have decided that the hamster is the pet for you (and determined whether you would like a golden hamster with long or short hair, or perhaps a dwarf), you should begin the search for your companion. Several options are available.

THE PET STORE

The most popular place for obtaining a hamster is the pet store. While many pet shops these days are opting not to sell puppies and kittens, most still carry small pocket pets, a group to which the hamster belongs.

Hamsters should generally be kept separately, in clean and spacious habitats.

The benefit of the pet shop is the convenience it presents. Find a good shop with a knowledgeable staff, and you can take advantage of one-stop shopping. This enables you to buy the hamster and necessary supplies for his care at the same location.

Look for a shop with a staff that can answer questions about the care of the pets they are placing. They should offer sound advice on hamster care and be able to tell the difference between male hamsters and females (a male's testicles are usually quite recognizable). The shop should be sanitary—evident in the animals' clean food and water and general lack of odor. The pets within the shop should look healthy and well-adjusted, their habitats clean and uncrowded.

These young siblings are being housed together.

Hamsters in the pet shop should, in most cases, be housed separately. The exceptions may be younger siblings, which may be housed together, and dwarf hamsters which are more social in nature than are their golden cousins and thus more amenable to cohabitation. The ideal, however, is separate housing, which indicates that the store understands the solitary nature of hamsters, and also reduces the risk that you'll discover an unexpected hamster pregnancy once you get your new pet home.

THE BREEDER

If you want a more exotic hamster—say, a teddy bear (longhaired) hamster of a specific color or pattern— then the breeder is usually your best bet. Hamster breeders may be difficult to locate in a given area, so you may have to do some hunting.

In your search for a hamster breeder, check the newspaper. Some advertise, and you may be able to find them easily. You may also want to ask the local pet shops that carry hamsters, as the breeders from whom they obtain their animals may breed exotic varieties. Ask local veterinarians, as well, especially those that treat hamsters. They should know breeders in the area who are their clients (this also shows that the breeder is willing to work with a veterinarian).

Another locale for finding breeders—especially several breeders all congregated together—is at a county or state fair. Hamsters are among the displays of the many animals that you will find at fairs. The individuals handling those hamsters are usually their breeders, most of whom couldn't be happier to speak with prospective buyers who appreciate the quality of fine show hamsters.

THE ANIMAL SHELTER

As part of that endless cycle of too many hamsters and not enough homes, some of those abandoned or homeless hamsters find themselves at the doorstep of the local animal shelter. What happens to them at that point depends on the shelter and the resources available to it.

Some shelters have set up hamster adoption programs and encourage would-be hamster owners to visit the many fine animals available for adoption. But others, because they are overwhelmed with the vast numbers of dogs and cats that come their way, have no choice but to humanely euthanize the small rodents. Unfortunately they simply do not have the staff, money or space to accommodate the hamsters. Contact your local shelters as possible sources for a hamster—and

A veterinarian is a good resource for finding a reputable hamster breeder.

consider the overcrowded pet population when thinking of breeding your pet.

Choosing a Healthy Hamster

Regardless of where you obtain your hamster, the criteria by which you choose your new pet should be
taken seriously. Whether purchasing a hamster from a
pet store, from a breeder at a county fair or from an
animal shelter, consider the following points when
evaluating potential pets.

AGE

No matter how you slice it, hamsters do not have long
life spans. Most live for two to three years.

Most people naturally prefer a younger hamster, as the
young pets' minimal experience with humans allows
the new owner to easily socialize him. This does not
mean an older hamster is out of the question, however.

An older hamster, with gentle handling, can bond to new people as
well, especially if his experience
with humans has been positive.

As for the older hamster, who may
have had negative experiences with
humans, you can enjoy a mutually
satisfying relationship with this animal, but on his terms. He may
never enjoy the handling that some
pets delight in, yet he can still partake in daily forays out of his enclo-
sure and take comfort in the fact that he is cared for
each day by an owner who does not force him into
uncomfortable situations. You in turn may take pride
in knowing that with this compassion you are rekin-
dling a hamster's faith in humans.

> **SIGNS OF A HEALTHY
> HAMSTER**
>
> Bright, lively eyes
>
> Clean, erect ears
>
> Well-formed and trimmed incisors
>
> Hearty appetite
>
> Barrel-shaped physique
>
> Alert expression

MALE OR FEMALE?

While hamsters exhibit differences in behavior during
mating, most veteran hamster owners do not see a

dramatic difference between the two as pets. This is probably because they are solitary animals and housed individually.

Here are some ways that you can determine the sex of a hamster: In the female, the distance between the anus and the sexual opening is much smaller than in the male. You can also see that the male has a more pointed rear end. After the fourth or fifth week (when the male hamster is sexually mature) the testicles are clearly visible on either side of the anus.

Curiosity is a good indicator of a healthy hamster.

While you may not have a preference from a hamster keeping perspective, gender can play an important role in unexpected pregnancies. You are best off working with breeders, pet shop staff and shelter personnel who are well-versed in telling males from females (which can be difficult in very young hamsters). To be safe, always follow the separate housing rule. If you house two hamsters together, you run the risk of ending up not only with an injured pet, but with an unplanned litter of hamsters.

PHYSICAL CONDITION

Health is of the utmost importance when choosing a hamster. A hamster that is healthy when you first bring him into your home is likely to live to an old age and remain in good health along the way. The opposite is likely true of the hamster that isn't a picture of health at the beginning.

When evaluating potential pets, look for the hamster with sparkling, lively eyes; clean ears held erect and alert; even, well-formed, well-trimmed incisors (the sign of a proper bite and healthy gnawing habits); and a proportioned, compact, barrel-shaped physique that exudes an aura of health.

Stress, diet and general care are also indicated by the condition of the hamster's coat. A healthy hamster's coat should have even fur and be clean (from his incessant self-grooming sessions), with no evidence of hair loss in a young hamster (some hair loss can be normal in an aging hamster). Even though the animal may not be inclined to climb right into your hand in the spirit of "love at first sight," the animal should demonstrate a fun-loving curiosity about his environment—especially about toys.

CLEAN BILL OF HEALTH

	HEALTHY HAMSTER	SICK HAMSTER
Eyes	Lively and shiny	Sticky discharge, puffy
Nose	Dry	Wet
Fur	Abundant and silky	Dull and course
Body	Cylindrical, filled out	Thin
Behavior	Vigorous	Lethargic, unresponsive

If you visit the hamster at noon and he seems rather listless and tired, don't simply assume that this lazy little animal obviously isn't the pet for you. Remember that this is a nocturnal creature that would rather be sleeping than impressing would-be owners at this time of day. Come back later in the afternoon or evening to witness his true character.

One thing to avoid is a hamster with a wet rear end. This is not likely caused by the hamster sitting in his water dish! The hamster may be afflicted by the severe bacterial hamster ailment, wet tail. If caught early, this can be treated with antibiotics and fluid therapy, but knowingly choosing a pet with the condition, and perhaps exposing other hamsters that you already own, can spell trouble, as wet tail is highly contagious.

Avoid purchasing any other hamsters from the same enclosure as they too may be affected.

Evaluate the hamster's environment as well. Stress can take a heavy toll on a hamster's health. You may not notice any outward signs of health problems in the hamster from a crowded, unclean enclosure, but a pet coming from such an environment will probably not live as long as one from a clean, stress-free habitat.

A stress-free environment, including a separate cage and a compassionate owner, is important to a hamster's health.

What Makes the Hamster Unique?

Indeed the hamster is unique among rodent pets. Consider some of the hamster's cousins, beginning with mice and rats. The hamster does not have centuries behind him of living in close proximity to humans (his history, as we have seen, is quite the opposite), yet despite this distinct difference, mice and rats actually have much in common with their hamster cousins.

Being rodents, mice, rats and hamsters all share chisel-like incisors that require constant gnawing for proper

37

maintenance, all thrive under similar living situations in captivity and eat the same basic diet. Mice, however, tend to be more timid than hamsters and rats, the latter two enjoying regular forays out of their cages with their human handlers—an activity that can prove frightening, even fatally stressful, for most mice. By the same token, hamsters are less gregarious and, with all due respect, not quite as intelligent as rats. Prospective owners seeking an easy-care rodent pet should therefore have a clear vision of what they are looking for in a rodent pet, and what they would rather avoid.

The hamster's button nose is a favorite trait.

The major difference between mice and rats and the hamster is an unexpected characteristic that has nothing to do with lifestyle or cohabitation. Yet for some would-be rodent owners this characteristic elevates the hamster instantly above the mouse and rat as the superior pet. That trait is the tail, or, more specifically, the hamster's lack thereof.

For all practical purposes, the pet hamster has no tail. Instead he has a short, tapered stub that contributes to the compact, cylindrical shape of the hamster's physique. This stubby rear end, the product of an underground burrowing existence, has helped kids convince mom and dad to grant permission for a rodent pet. One look at that little creature *sans* tail next to the rats and mice in the pet shop and parents find themselves saying yes to the hamster.

Of course there is more to the hamster than the lack of a tail. Once new owners get past the tail issue, they discover a small pet with a gentle, sweet temperament (if properly handled and socialized), coupled with an appearance that sets him apart as a unique individual among rodent pets.

This individuality is most vividly reflected in the hamster's face and head. His senses of smell and hearing have been largely responsible for the hamster's survival in his native territory. The hamster's eyes are large and expressive, complementing his pink button nose and perky rounded ears that are perched erect, yet slightly askew, at the top of the head.

The combination of these sensory characteristics lend the hamster a distinct expression of whimsy and fun. Hence the hamster is seen as more cute than he is beautiful. The hamster's chubby, almost jowly, cheeks engineered for food storage invite caricature as does his habit of sitting up on his hind legs, munching on a treat that he holds in his delicate, surprisingly dexterous hands. Most devoted owners could gaze upon such an idyllic scene for hours.

Living

with a

part two

Hamster

chapter 4

Bringing Your
Hamster
Home

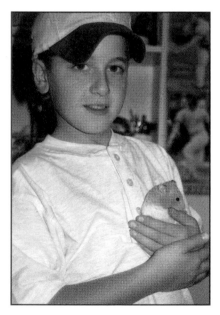

Making Preparations

Once you have decided that the hamster is the pet for you, some preparations are necessary. Purchasing a hamster on impulse because you spot a darling little cream-colored teddy bear that wiggles her whiskers at you as you pass by a pet shop is not the wise way to go. Before you take the plunge, take some time to think about the commitment you would be making, even to what is a relatively inexpensive pet, and carry on with that commitment in mind.

The first step, once you have determined to share your life for the next three years or so with a hamster, is to take stock of what you will need to provide a safe and secure home for your pet. You will need to assemble her habitat (see chapter 5); stock up on food; and purchase bedding, food and water receptacles, as well as a selection of toys and exercise equipment. Then you will have to decide where to place your hamster's habitat.

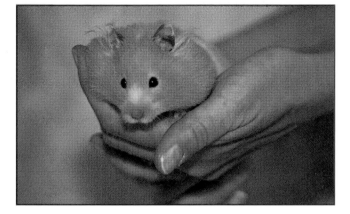

Hamsters are cute, inexpensive, take little space and are easy to keep clean.

Leaving the environment to which she has become accustomed can be a dangerously stressful experience for a hamster. Ease your hamster's anxiety by taking care of the details long before you bring your new pet home.

If the hamster is destined for a home with children, which is the norm for this animal that is considered a wonderful children's pet, by all means involve the kids in the preparation process, but remember that a hamster must never be relegated to the sole care of a child. While these easy-care pets provide kids with a fine opportunity to learn and experience the responsibility of caring for a helpless creature, even the most dependable kids have been known to sleep on the job from time to time. Parents must remain involved to ensure that the hamster continues to receive the optimum care she requires.

THINGS YOU NEED BEFORE YOUR HAMSTER COMES HOME

- Habitat
- Food and water plus containers for these
- Toys and exercise equipment
- Bedding material
- Name of a reliable veterinarian

Finally, enjoy the anticipation. Working together, purchasing the equipment, preparing a new pet's home, learning the ins and outs of proper care—there are few joys in life more thrilling for kids and adults alike. Take it slow, proceed with common sense and you are sure to make the arrival of your new pet a truly memorable experience for the entire family.

Get to know the special characteristics of your new hamster, including requirements for physical exercise and mental stimulation.

QUALITY VETERINARY SERVICES

Before you bring your new pet home, you should take the time to find a veterinarian. Ask other hamster owners for references, then visit two or three clinics to get a feel for the practice. You need to find a veterinarian who has experience, equipment, drugs and a trained staff for small animals. This includes a working knowledge of diseases and responses to medications that hamsters may have, as well as dietary needs, behavior and reproduction. Along with this level of expertise, look for the availability of emergency or after-hours service. Your hamster will benefit from a veterinarian who is familiar and comfortable with treating the medical problems of small and exotic animals. The first stop before you take your new hamster home should be a visit to the veterinarian so you can get a baseline evaluation of the hamster's health.

Welcoming Your New Pet Home

Common sense should prevail when that grand day arrives. You are ready to pick up your pet and bring her home. The habitat is clean and organized, fresh food and water await, a layer of clean bedding sits ready to invite the attentions of a burrowing little creature and the toys are ready for play.

This day provides you with the ideal time to begin earning your new hamster's respect. Work toward this ultimate goal from your first meeting, and you just might be rewarded with a bond between pet and owner that you find quite surprising.

When you pick up your hamster, bring a small ventilated container with you for transport of your new pet. Most stores will have these available, but again, you want to be prepared. If the trip will be a short one (which is preferable), a heavy cardboard box with holes for ventilation will suffice. But to prevent the hamster from attempting an escape by chewing, a heavier plastic, also well-ventilated container may be superior. This latter item will also come in handy down the road as a "holding pen" for the hamster when you are cleaning her cage.

Pictured are travel supplies for your hamster: a well-ventilated container, food and water, bedding and some toys.

Place some bedding material in this small travel box— if possible some bedding from the hamster's enclosure at the pet shop, shelter or breeding facility—to provide not only a comfortable ride, but a familiar scent, as well. Stash a couple of treats in your pocket, too, perhaps a peanut in the shell or a sunflower seed to offer your new pet and keep her occupied for the journey home.

After visiting the veterinarian, take the hamster directly to her new home. Don't stop off at a party first or visit a child's classroom to show off the new pet. Keep the animal's well-being and the alleviation of her stress in mind. Your job is to get your hamster home as soon as possible, place her in her new home and then leave her alone for a while to get accustomed to her surroundings.

Assuming you have already wisely placed the hamster's habitat in a quiet, untraveled corner of the house, once home, the hamster will probably explore the new enclosure a bit, check out her food, and perhaps burrow into some shavings for a little nap to recover from the journey. Providing the hamster with the opportunity to partake of these simple introductory acts is your first step toward earning your new pet's lifelong respect.

KEEPING CLEAN

Hamsters often appear to have a coat full of cage bedding or litter. They are, after all, little balls of nocturnal energy. In order to remove the debris, hamsters can be combed with a soft brush or you can "pet" off the particles. Cage bedding should be changed twice a week and bathroom material at least every other day. Disinfect and carefully rinse all washable toys, as well as food and water receptacles, weekly.

Gentle Hamster Handling

Take your time in interacting with your new hamster. Even if she seems ready for play, introduce yourself gradually. You will both benefit in the long run.

Hamsters navigate through their world by relying primarily on their senses of smell and hearing. During your first few days together, allow her to get acquainted with your voice and your scent. Do this by speaking softly to the hamster when you approach her enclosure for daily feedings, water changes, toy rotations (just like children, hamsters thrive with an ever-changing variety of playthings) and the daily removal of soiled bedding.

All the family members can introduce themselves this way, but try to keep your brief interactions to a minimum. Do your hamster a favor and reserve these interactions only for the animal's family members in the beginning. The kids may be tempted to invite everyone in the neighborhood over to meet the family's new hamster, but explain that it's better to wait a few days to let her get adjusted to her immediate family. Once you build that important foundation of respect, the hamster should be amenable to meeting outsiders and probably friendlier in doing so, as well.

When you believe the hamster is ready for you to do so, gently reach your hand into her habitat, an act that will invite the animal to approach and sniff your skin. If treated gently, most hamsters are not biters by nature. If your new pet tries to take a little nip of your finger while exploring your hand, either she isn't ready for such an intrusion or she may have caught a whiff of your lunch lingering on your fingertips.

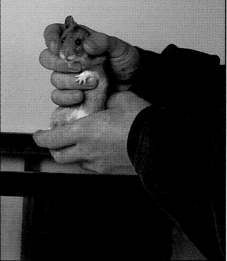

You will further earn your hamster's esteem by reserving these initial interactions to the late afternoon and early evening when this nocturnal creature shakes off her daytime sleepiness and emerges energetic and ready for activity. If you awaken the animal constantly during the day when she is trying to sleep, the hamster will likely become frustrated with this new, and rather inconsiderate, human in her life. Waking a soundly sleeping hamster, even one known for a docile disposition, could incite a bite that must not be blamed on hamster nastiness, but owner negligence and disrespect.

Wrap your fingers gently but confidently around the hamster's body, then lift her out of the cage.

HOLDING YOUR HAMSTER

After those first few days of quiet introductions, your hamster is ready for the next step—being handled.

47

Proceed gradually. Before lifting the hamster out of her enclosure, speak softly to alert her to your presence. Next, gently place your hand into her enclosure as she has become accustomed to your doing.

When approaching your hamster, there are several things to keep in mind for your own safety. Leave your hamster alone if she rolls over on her back and bares her teeth. This is a signal that she is feeling defensive or threatened. You should also respect her space if she runs from your hand or makes a squealing or guttural sound. Also remember to leave a sleeping hamster to her nap instead of waking her. Most of all never squeeze, pinch or roughly handle your hamster.

While technically hamsters can be lifted by the excess skin at the napes of their necks, it is better to simply wrap your fingers gently yet firmly around her barrel-shaped body and lift her up. Use your other hand to offer extra support at the hamster's rear end and hold the animal close to your body.

If your hamster loves to speed around the cage and playfully dart out of your grasp, try this tip: Create a wall by putting the palms of your hands together, and the hamster will generally run into the wall, letting you close your hands around her body.

During initial outings and whenever children handle the hamster, make sure the hamster is held close over a surface such as a table or the floor to prevent injuries if she falls. By the same token, never leave the hamster alone on a table or elevated surface. To do so is to invite disaster for your pet who, due to her insatiable curiosity, could be seriously injured.

Handling your hamster with respect and a quiet demeanor will instill in the animal a sense of security

SAFE HAMSTER HANDLING

Here are some ways to gently pick up your hamster:

- If you are unaccustomed to holding a hamster, you can take advantage of your hamster's curiosity by holding a small box or empty soup can in front of her. Your hamster will most likely venture inside the container to check it out, and you can then pick her up.

- Cup your hands together such that one hand is beneath your hamster and the other creates a roof that hides the hamster between your hands.

and positive association with being handled and, as an offshoot, toward her new human family members. Your pet will recognize when she is being treated with respect and will learn quickly whom she may trust. Introduce yourself gradually and gently, observe those preliminary safety precautions when handling the animal and you will earn a trustworthy reputation.

Hamster Habits

First-time hamster owners are usually surprised at all there is to learn about the species when a hamster joins the family. Much of this can be learned simply by observing the hamster and heeding her signals.

GROOMING

Watch your hamster regularly and you will soon realize that this little animal grooms herself constantly. Before eating, after eating, before a nap, after a nap, before a spin in the hamster ball, after a spin in the hamster ball—the hamster stops, straightens any dis-

Grooming with a soft brush helps remove bedding dust and is a great way to bond with your pet.

placed hairs and washes her face for the seventeenth time that day. Indeed this is a meticulously clean little pet, so diligent about cleanliness, both her own and her habitat's, that she could be christened the Felix Unger of the rodent world.

Though some owners may view such habits as a sign that the hamster requires grooming by her owners, that is an incorrect notion. The hamster is perfectly capable of taking care of her own grooming, no doubt a skill sculpted by her solitary life in the wild where, in the absence of other hamsters to join in sessions of mutual grooming, the hamster

49

learned to groom on her own. This has more to do with survival than with vanity, as a healthy coat is critical to protecting the hamster from climactic extremes.

As a rule, hamsters should not be bathed. Because their grooming routines serve to cleanse them naturally—and because they are essentially odorless by nature—there is no need for a human-style bath. Owners should forego bathing their hamster because bathing can be too stressful; that stress can lead to a sick hamster. Hamsters are especially prone to respiratory problems, so it is best to avoid the potential chill a bath can cause, which, when combined with the stress of the experience, can cause illness.

Always look for physical changes in your hamster.

If you still feel inclined to assist your hamster in her grooming regimen, you can do so by brushing the animal gently with a soft toothbrush. Most hamsters are amenable to short brushing sessions that can also help remove bedding dust or other habitat residue that may cling to the hair.

While not critical to hamster health and beauty, short brushing sessions do offer you a chance to share some "quality" time enjoying your hamster. At the same time, they provide you with the opportunity to observe your pet more closely for any new or developing physical changes that could indicate illness or injury. For instance, while running the soft brush over the hamster's tummy, you may notice a lump that wasn't there before, or spot a damp area on the rear end that could signal the illness wet tail. Note such signs at their onset, and contact the veterinarian before a potentially serious condition progresses to more dangerous, perhaps untreatable, stages.

chapter 5

Housing

Your **Hamster**

When it comes to home, hamsters are determined homebodies, never content unless they are living in the ultimate hamster domicile with everything in its place and all corners squeaky clean. Yet the hamster, even the happy hamster, is the consummate escape artist. Escape is seen as a grand game, reminiscent of what sent wild hamsters over miles and miles of desert terrain in search of food and adventure. The challenge is to place your hamster in an enclosure without even the tiniest possible escape route—such as an ill-fitting top or a tiny hole that can be gnawed.

Hamster Habitats

The goal of the hamster owner is to provide the hamster with a home so attractive, well-furnished and clean, that the animal won't need to entertain the possibility of escape. The good news is that meeting this goal is quite simple.

The ideal hamster habitat has separate areas for sleeping and eating, a bathroom and play space.

The important elements to understand in optimum hamster housing is that this animal requires cleanliness as well as neatness. He will only rest when everything within his environment is arranged with a distinct spot for eating, drinking and sleeping; another section for playing; and another designated as a bathroom. Consequently, the rule of thumb in hamster housing is that bigger is better.

Various types of housing exist for these animals, and opinions vary widely on which is best. But all veteran hamster keepers agree that one should strive to provide the hamster with as much room as possible, at least 19 square inches. A roomy enclosure offers you the opportunity to design the interior with all the separate areas for the hamster's various life functions.

Set up the hamster's home before ever bringing your new pet home—set up the sleeping area, the bathroom, the eating and play areas and cover the floor with bedding.

THE GLASS OR PLASTIC
AQUARIUM-STYLE TANK

A popular setup for hamster keeping—and one in which you will most often find pets displayed—is the glass aquarium. (A variation on this is a plastic version that comes fully equipped with a ventilated handle top and other internal accessories.) For a single hamster, the aquarium tank should be at least 10 gallons in size, it must be well constructed (no sharp edges at the corners, no cracked sides) and it must have a well-fitting top with no gaps or holes that can inspire escape.

The best top for an aquarium setup is a closely meshed screen top framed with metal that slides on and off.

This type ensures not only security—the hamster, skilled as he may be, cannot slide the properly installed top off—but it also provides ventilation, which is critical to hamster health.

Another style of tank setup provides even more ventilation because it boasts a screen top as well as one side of screen. The mesh of the screening on any hamster home must be woven closely enough to prevent the injury of tiny hamster toes, and it must be free of tears that could be enlarged by a hamster bent on escape.

The benefits of aquarium-style housing are that it is easy to clean; keeps odors at bay; and retains hay, bedding, food and residual dust within the hamster's house (and prevents it from overwhelming yours). Furthermore, if the enclosure is properly roofed, this style of hamster home keeps the hamster safe and confined, yet quite visible to the many admirers who will want to come and observe the little fellow as he plays, eats and naps.

Hamsters are opportunistic escape artists, and it is wise to check your pet's enclosure frequently for escape possibilities.

The owner should be aware that there can be a potential lack of ventilation with this tank. In other words, because it is enclosed, the owner must check the cleanliness frequently as there will not be an odor that indicates it's cleaning time. The tank may prevent the dissemination of odors throughout the household at large, but it must be cleaned often to maintain the hamster's health.

An aquarium tank should be at least 10 gallons in size, with no sharp edges at the corners, no cracked sides and a well-fitting top with no gaps or holes.

THE TRADITIONAL WIRE CAGE

While countless hamster keepers swear by the aquarium-style hamster house, there are just as many who would choose nothing other than a traditional wire cage. Ventilation, they claim, is the number one reason for doing so, and indeed a roomy, airy enclosure helps prevent respiratory illness in resident hamsters.

As with any choice of hamster domicile, the cage must be well made and free of exposed wires or tears that could lead to injury and/or escape. The floor should be solid to hold in bedding and to facilitate burrowing, and the door should be one that can be latched securely. Even though this design is obviously light and airy, this does not mean that you may forego the routine cleaning. Any style of housing must be cleaned regularly (more on how to go about that later), and the wire cage is no exception.

One trend in cages that is best avoided is the double-decker design. While such a setup is considered ideal for the hamster's larger cousin, the chinchilla, it can

Living with
a Hamster

prove dangerous for the small hamster, which is not as adept at climbing (he is a burrower, after all). He could take a serious tumble from the higher reaches of such a cage. Stick with the traditional single-story design and make life safer for your pet.

TUBE SETUPS

Although it is often referred to generically as a Habitrail, there are various brands of this unique hamster setup that imitates the hamster's natural underground environment. The setup is a configuration of plastic tubes, compartments and similar segments that an owner assembles in various arrangements, enabling the hamster to climb through a maze not all that different from the vast burrows and tunnels hamsters inhabit in the wild.

Some owners prefer to keep their hamster in a traditional tank and provide external tubes for a playtime treat.

This setup is a delightfully fun environment for a hamster because it satisfies the small rodent's natural instincts to burrow and travel through narrow tunnels, but it has drawbacks as well. Cleaning, for one, can be a challenge, in that the unit must be disassembled to clean the various segments thoroughly—and reassembled once cleaning is done. Failure to clean it properly results in an overpowering smell from urine and bits of food left in the various reaches of the habitat.

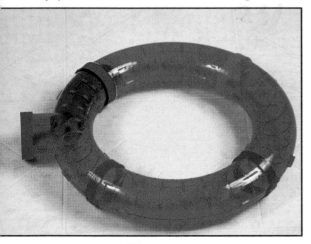

Another drawback is that hamsters have been known to chew through the plastic of these systems, which can obviously cause a variety of problems. The hamster can escape, he can suffer digestive upset and the results of his efforts can prove economically costly to the owner.

Many hamster owners have devised a compromise, in which the tube setup is used not as a hamster's primary residence, but as a supplement to the primary residence. In this way, the hamster can eat and sleep in his more traditional cage or tank, and then enjoy playtime in the tube habitat. Such a combination provides the hamster—and his owner—with the best of both worlds.

HOMEMADE ENCLOSURES

Most veteran hamster keepers recommend that owners steer clear of homemade hamster habitats. Unless you are an expert on rodent behavior and physiology and how these animals interact with various materials they might find in their environment, you are wise to rely on those who are, and choose a commercially made product that will prove to be safer and more secure for the hamster.

Commercial enclosures of gnaw-proof glass, metal or wire are superior to a homemade wooden structure—and less expensive in the long run. Stick with the more traditional setups, and avoid any unexpected, not to mention easily prevented, tragedies.

Bedding material, food and water containers, treats (such as sunflower seeds), an exercise wheel and toys are some essentials for the hamster cage.

Additional Supplies

There is far more to the ideal hamster habitat than walls alone. The furnishings within those walls are just as vital to keeping the hamster healthy and mentally stimulated.

There are several items that you'll want to have on hand before you bring your hamster home: a water bottle or dish, a food dish, nesting/bedding material, an exercise wheel and/or ball and some toys. You also need to have a supply of food ready for your new friend as discussed in chapter 6.

WATER BOTTLE

Hamsters need to have fresh water available at all times. Pet stores sell various sizes of water bottles; it is recommended to keep a medium-size bottle in your hamster's cage. To ensure that the water is always fresh, you should change the water in the bottle daily. When you clean the bottle, be sure that it is well rinsed of all traces of soap. If the bottle gets too dirty, it is time to get a new one. Some hamsters like to use a water dish, but end up sitting in the water and dirtying it or tipping the dish over altogether.

There are several types of bird dishes available that fasten securely to the side of the cage. Using this type of dish will help prevent your hamster from tipping his water, but you must make sure that the dish is fastened low enough for the hamster to reach. Some owners place the water dish directly under the water bottle to catch drips and prevent soaked bedding.

FOOD DISHES

Hamsters tend to enjoy sitting in their food dishes as well as eating from them, so a weighted dish is recommended. The bowl that you get for your hamster should be large enough to hold an ample supply of food for their daily energy needs. Make sure the dish is shallow enough that your hamster can reach the food at the bottom.

BEDDING

The choice and type of bedding you choose for your hamster is crucial to his well-being. This is, after all, a burrowing animal that takes great pleasure in digging into a mound of bedding for a nap, for a game or for hiding a litter of newborns. Your choice of bedding is not only directly connected to the hamster's pleasure in this, but also to his overall health.

While hamsters are burrowing animals, this does not mean you need to re-create his natural environment in your home. Avoid the temptation to carpet the floor of the hamster's enclosure with a thick layer of natural materials through which he can burrow and build his own maze of tunnels. These materials can actually prove to be *too* natural, containing parasites, bacteria and other disease-carrying agents that could prove deadly to the resident hamster.

Nesting material should be clean, dry and non-toxic—covering 2 to 3 inches of the habitat floor.

Bedding should be clean, dry, nontoxic and absorbent. The most popular bedding choice, and one that typically satisfies this criteria, is wood shavings. Avoid cedar shavings, as this aromatic wood can prove too intense to small rodents, and opt instead for pine or aspen. These must be shavings that are produced specifically for the care of small animals; don't carpet the enclosure with remnants from a lumber yard or woodworking shop. The hamster can suffer severe repercussions from the dust and chemicals in the wood. Similar problems can arise from cat litter, another inappropriate bedding choice for hamsters.

Other bedding options include products made from vegetable materials and shredded paper. Should you choose the paper option, avoid newspaper. The ink can be toxic. Plain, unprinted newspaper stock or another type of similarly plain paper is a better option.

You may supplement the bedding with a few handfuls of hay. Like everything you place in your hamster's habitat, the hay, too, must be clean, dry and free of parasites and mold. Place the hay in one section of the enclosure to designate the nesting area.

Regardless of the type you choose, cover the floor of the hamster's habitat with 2 or 3 inches of clean, fresh bedding. This will provide your pet with ample room in which to burrow, play and hide. If you carpet the floor with a generous layer of bedding and keep it clean, you're maintaining a sound foundation for all other furnishings in the hamster's abode.

HIDEAWAYS (NEST BOXES)

As a nocturnal creature—and as a small rodent—the hamster must have somewhere to hide from the prying eyes of his admirers. Provide your pet with a variety of beds in which he can build a cozy nest.

The choice of these items must be made with hamster physiology in mind. Remember those teeth and their shredding ability, and keep away from any materials that could fall victim to chewing. Soft plastic and cardboard, for example, won't last long with a hamster about. Hard plastic, PVC piping and the various items made specifically for hamster habitats are superior choices—and less expensive in the long run because they don't need to be constantly replaced.

Position one or two of these nest boxes in the hamster's home—preferably some distance away from the food dishes and the water bottle, as these should occupy their own specific spots within the habitat. The hamster tends to designate a particular corner of his domicile as a bathroom. Once you figure out just where this is, position food, water and nest boxes away from that area, and foster the hamster's desire for order and cleanliness.

As for the nest/hiding boxes themselves, a variety of styles exist. You may want to provide your hamster with two choices to offer him a bit of variety. Your hamster may enjoy, for example, one box with solid walls in which he can hide completely from the outside world, and another with clear hard plastic walls and several different openings that he can use as a make-shift playhouse.

The best nest hideaways are those that provide the hamster with an accessible door opening and plenty of privacy once the hamster is inside, some of which are available commercially (you may find smaller models for dwarf hamsters as these are becoming more popular). Some of these are traditional box shapes, and others come in a variety of styles, designs and shapes to keep a hamster interested and entertained. Most commercial styles are composed of safe, non-toxic materials that can withstand long-term rodent gnawing.

HAMSTER TOYS
Exercise wheel
Hamster ball
Play ladders and bridges
Varied toys for climbing
Cardboard cylinders
PVC piping

Some household items can also be used as hamster hideaways— although these are usually temporary because of the materials involved. An empty tissue box or cylindrical oatmeal container, for example, can provide the hamster with a fun change of pace, but because these items are made of cardboard, they probably won't last long. Use your imagination when seeking out household items for your pet, but always keep the basic rules of hamster safety in mind.

PROPER TOYS

Hamsters are very active and thrive on stimulation. They enjoy interactions both with their owners and new and exciting items within their environment.

Offer your pet a variety of toys, all of which must be well-constructed and made of nontoxic materials. The classic hamster toy is the exercise wheel, but running on the wheel can be addictive, not to mention noisy for the owner when the hamster runs all night. By all means give your hamster a wheel to run on, but offer him other toys as well.

Supplement the wheel with several other toys. The hamster ball—a hollow plastic ball into which a hamster may securely sit and "run" through the house safely—is a favorite, as are commercially available ladders, bridges and novelty hideaways that may be used for hiding and climbing. A variety of common household items are also available for play purposes, such as cardboard toilet paper or paper towel rolls and remnants of PVC piping, both of which the hamster may use for a rousing game of hide-and-seek.

Fruit tree branches and chunks of wood for gnawing are also fun for the hamster and at the same time attractive additions to the hamster habitat. They not only provide the animal with a new and different surface on which to climb, but also a delectable gnawing item. To protect the hamster, make sure that the wood or branch is clean, untreated and nontoxic. You can buy pieces from well-stocked pet supply stores.

Alternating different toys gives the hamster something new to explore and climb on.

Safety should, as always, be first on your mind when choosing hamster toys. Make sure the toys are the right size for your hamster, such as smaller hamster balls and wheels for dwarfs and larger items for goldens. Check the wheel regularly, too, to ensure it remains in good working order, with no exposed wires or sharp edges

that could hurt the toes or tummy of a particularly ath-
letic hamster, or catch the long hair of a teddy bear
hamster.

When placing new toys within your hamster's abode
(which you should do periodically, replacing familiar
items with new exciting ones and rotating the toys
every day or two to retain your pet's interest), make
sure the toys sit securely in the flooring material so as
not to roll over or fall onto a hamster should he use it
in a way that was not intended.

*This hamster
car is a great
variation of the
exercise ball.*

Household Upkeep

Regardless of the particular housing you choose, your
pet's home must be cleaned regularly and thoroughly.
A clean cage will keep your hamster happy and active
as well as in good health.

First, soiled bedding should be removed daily from the
enclosure, which is typically quite simple because most
hamsters will designate one specific corner of their
enclosure as the bathroom. Simply remove the
affected material and you have done your job.

Uneaten food should also be removed each day, which
may prove a bit more of a challenge. It's not unusual
for a hamster with an excess of food to fill his ample
cheek pouches and bury his treasure somewhere
within the bedding, perhaps in his nest box or beneath
a favorite toy. If your hamster has this traditional habit,

try to find his cache, clean it out and thus prevent a buildup of odor from the natural decomposition of food.

In addition to daily maintenance, the bedding should be completely removed and replaced every week. When it comes time to do this, place the resident hamster in an established holding cage or box—a small, secure enclosure equipped with a bit of bedding and a toy or two as well as some food for the hamster's comfort (you can also use this holding cage for trips to the veterinarian or for family travels). As with the main enclosure, make sure the holding cage is clean and escape proof.

With your hamster safely confined and out of the way, carry on with the cleaning. Remove all the items from the cage, and clean everything with warm water and mild soap or detergent. Dispose of the bedding from the enclosure, and thoroughly clean the walls and the floor (or the segments of the tube setup) with warm water and mild soap. Avoid strong detergents or cleaning solvents that can irritate the hamster's respiratory tract or prove to be toxic if not completely rinsed away. Rinse the soap from the enclosure thoroughly—you want to be rid of every bit of soap residue—and then dry the surfaces just as thoroughly.

Thorough cleaning of your hamster's cage every week is essential to maintaining the health and well-being of your pet.

Once the enclosure is dry, carpet the floor with a new fresh 2- or 3-inch layer of bedding, replace the cage furnishings and, finally, replace the resident hamster.

Where to Place the Habitat?

Basic maintenance of your hamster's habitat is critical, but so is the placement of that enclosure. First, the hamster must reside indoors. Since the wild hamster spent a great deal of time underground, the hamster simply does not do well exposed to the elements, especially when those elements involve extreme temperatures, precipitation and the threat of unwelcome visitors. A layer of bedding will not suffice in keeping the hamster protected from these elements, so keep him indoors where he will remain physically safe and emotionally secure.

HAMSTER NIGHTLIFE

The nocturnal nature of the hamster should be kept in mind when you decide where to place the habitat within your house. The hamster that is allowed to follow his own natural rhythms will sleep during the day and play at night. Therefore, place his enclosure in a section of the house that is quiet, dimly lit and protected from the traffic of the family's daily activities.

Limit the stress your hamster may experience from the attention of other household pets.

When the hamster awakens full of energy and ready to play in the afternoon or early evening, make sure he has toys and food to enjoy. This is also the perfect opportunity for you to take the hamster out of his enclosure for some interactions with his family or for a romp in his tube habitat.

As the evening progresses, you must also think of your own sleep patterns. You can remedy the squeaking wheel situation—and ensure you get a good night's sleep yourself—by placing the hamster's cage far enough away from your own sleeping area and providing the animal with a variety of toys so he doesn't become addicted to the wheel.

TEMPERATURE REQUIREMENTS

The enclosure should remain safely out of direct sunlight at all times. Heat and exposure to direct sun can be extremely harmful to your hamster's health. When evaluating where your hamster's cage should sit, keep in mind that the sunlight will change during the day, so a shaded spot by a window in the morning could be flooded with sun in the afternoon.

Avoid drafts, as well, either from open windows or air-conditioning vents. Drafts are particularly dangerous to hamsters, as they can contribute to respiratory problems. The ideal draft-free temperature for hamsters is anywhere from 65 to 80 degrees Fahrenheit (for newborn hamsters the ideal temperature is 70 to 75 degrees). Though they are desert dwellers by nature, they thrive best in the same basic room temperatures preferred by humans.

HAMSTER-PROOFING

Make sure that no particularly dangerous household items are within reach of the cage, and thus the hamster, either. You certainly don't want electrical cords hanging into the enclosure that could be inviting to the hamster's gnawing habits, nor do you want your pet's home to be situated near cleaning solvents or similar chemical agents with fumes that could prove damaging to the hamster's sensitive respiratory tract.

Finally, make sure the enclosure is in a safe place. He should be situated out of the reach of other household pets, such as cats and dogs, that may not be able to physically harm the hamster, but whose mere presence outside of the enclosure is enough to cause stress.

Here are some other dangerous situations that you should protect your hamster from:

- Open doors that can close suddenly, catching and squashing your hamster.

- Pointed objects can tear cheek pouches if stored away.

- Overexposure to the sun can cause heatstroke.

- Watch for nibbling. Some plants are poisonous, often fatal, if digested.

- Be on your toes! You can step on your hamster if he is not supervised.

- Ventilation shafts provide the perfect opportunity for your hamster to escape.

- Hot objects (such as a toaster or curling iron) can burn your hamster.

- Inhaling stain and varnish can make your hamster ill and are toxic if ingested.

- Drawers and closets can suffocate your hamster if he is closed in.

Caring for Dwarf Hamsters

It is important that dwarf hamsters are housed together, in pairs. Once you have paired two, they should not be separated. These hamsters mate for life and experience difficulty adjusting to a new partner. If you do not want to end up with a litter of hamsters, you can select two females or two males to keep together (preferably starting at a young age).

THE CAGE

It is essential that you choose a secure cage for your dwarf hamsters; since they are so tiny, they make excellent escape artists! An aquarium or plastic tank with a mesh lid is a safe choice. Keep in mind that dwarfs require more space then Syrian hamsters, so choose a larger cage accordingly. Nesting material and wood shavings should be put in the cage as well as food and water bowls. Like all hamsters, dwarfs love exercise and need the smallest wheel possible for running.

HEALTH CARE

Dwarf hamsters are known for their excellent health. As a matter of fact, it is unusual for them to manifest illness until old age (their life span is between eighteen months and two years). As dwarf hamsters age, some suffer from cancer. Unfortunately, the tumors that they get are inoperable because of their small size. As long as the hamster seems comfortable, you can continue to care for him. When his condition begins to deteriorate, it is time to have him put to sleep. Another condition of old age in dwarf hamsters is cataracts. In this condition, the eyes start to look an opaque gray or white color. Cataracts will not cause the hamster pain, so it will most likely live the rest of its normal life span in relative comfort.

chapter 6

Feeding
Your
Hamster

The ease with which one can provide a hamster with a healthy, well-balanced diet is one of the reasons this animal is considered such an easy-care pet. Though she requires access to her food at all times, supplying that food is so simple even a young child can take on the duty (with parental supervision, of course).

Nutritional Needs

While we are inclined to think of the hamster as the quintessential vegetarian, in the wild the hamster enjoys a quite variegated—and rather omnivorous—diet. In addi-

tion to feasting on the vegetation products she finds during her nightly forays into her desert environment, she may supplement her diet with insects and any other meat-based items she happens to find.

Vegetarian Diet?

Many hamster owners acquire these animals because of their classically vegetarian diets, and you, the owner of the domestic hamster, need not mimic the carnivorous aspect of the wild hamster's diet by supplying your pet with meat or insects. To satisfy the hamster's daily protein needs, in which proteins should comprise approximately 15 to 20 percent of the diet, some hamster keepers promote the idea that you can supplement the animal's diet with mealworms. This is not necessary, however, and can actually cause digestive problems for the species that far outweigh any nutritional benefits mealworms present—nutritional benefits that can be garnered far easier from other food sources.

A safer and easier method of supplying hamsters with animal-based protein is to offer the animals a bit of cooked meat from time to time, but even this is not a necessary component of the healthy hamster diet. Feel free to offer your hamster a classically vegetarian diet, but be sure to vary what you feed her.

If you choose to avoid feeding your hamster meat, you can provide protein by feeding her some milk products. A teaspoon of yogurt or cottage cheese mixed with fruit is a healthy alternative. Remember to wait until the food is at room temperature before feeding it to your hamster. Provide small portions to avoid spoilage.

FEEDING YOUR HAMSTER

Feeding your hamster is a simple task, just follow the guidelines and ask your veterinarian if you have any concerns.

- varied diet consisting of a mix of commercially prepared food and fresh vegetables

- food available at all times

- constant supply of fresh, clean water

- healthful treats in moderation

Safe and Nutritious Foods

Here is a list of yummy food options that you can feed your hamster. Don't forget to provide fresh, high quality food that has been rinsed thoroughly. Dry food and water should be provided throughout the day and evening since hamsters love to snack.

Sprouts	Mealworms
Dandelion leaves	Meat
Corn (cob to gnaw on)	Sunflower seeds
Cooked or raw potato	Apple
White bread	Carrot
Boiled Rice	Lettuce (Iceberg)
Pasta	Meadow hay
Dog Biscuits	Cauliflower
Egg	Tomatoes
Cottage cheese	Banana
Yogurt	Strawberries
Chicken	Grapes
Cooked Fish	Berries

THE BASIC COMPONENTS

Like all mammals, the hamster requires a balanced diet composed of the basic nutrients: carbohydrates, fats, proteins, vitamins, minerals and plenty of fresh, clean water. The most efficient way to supply your pet with these nutrients is in a diet that combines commercially prepared hamster foods that are readily available at pet supply stores with fresh foods that are readily available in your own kitchen.

COMMERCIAL DIETS

Thanks to the popularity of pocket pets and the knowledge of their nutritional needs, there are a variety of commercial products on the market that please both the hamster's palette and the owner's desire for convenient feeding practices.

Basic seed mixtures are the first and more traditional of the commercially prepared foods. Most hamsters are thrilled with a mix of seeds, but if served as the sole dietary source, this will probably not provide the animal with a complete balance of nutrients. If the hamster chooses not to partake of all the ingredients, she will not get a complete balance, even though the mix represents a balanced diet.

A basic seed mix should be combined with other foods, such as fresh vegetables, to provide a complete diet for your hamster.

It's not at all unusual for a particularly finicky hamster to choose to feast only on sunflower seeds or only on some other type of seed she finds in the mix. Because no one food, especially no one seed, is the perfect food, eating only one component of a balanced diet will lead to malnutrition. If that ingredient happens to be a seed, she is also in danger of obesity, as seeds and nuts are very high in fat. In moderation, they are a fine component of the diet, but they are not appropriate as the sole component.

Pelleted or block-type food products are another type of commercial diet that prevents the problems of the seed mixture. Within the pellets and blocks are combined all the nutrients the hamster requires for a complete and balanced diet, and the hamster has no possibility of picking and choosing what she wants to eat and what she doesn't. Many of the block diets present an added bonus: Their hard consistency helps keep the teeth trimmed, maintaining the hamster's dental health while nourishing her at the same time.

FOODS TO AVOID

Canned or frozen vegetables; uncooked beans; green parts of potatoes and tomatoes; sprouting potatoes.

Because the seed mixture is generally tastier and more interesting to the hamster than the pelleted and block-type concoctions, the seed mixture is best fed in addition to the pellets or blocks to ensure the hamster both enjoys her meal and receives a proper mix of nutrients. If you happen to have a hamster that prefers seeds, however, you may need to wait to offer the seed mixture until after the hamster has ingested a ration of pellets or blocks.

A block-type food mix is a good way to provide your hamster with necessary nutrients.

In addition to providing a hamster with her complete nutrition, commercial diets are further beneficial in that they are readily available at most pet supply stores and they can be easily stored. Resist the temptation to stock up on these foods, however, because even though they boast relatively long shelf lives, they can still go bad.

When purchased in modest amounts and stored correctly—preferably in plastic airtight containers with secure lids—commercial hamster food should remain fresh and clean for weeks. If, however, you notice the supply has become moldy, stale or otherwise less than ideal, do not offer it to your hamster. Dispose of the supply and replace it with a fresh batch.

Fresh foods can also help keep your pet interested in her food, and thus help ensure she receives a full,

73

well-balanced complement of nutrients. Most hamsters love nothing more than to go to the food dish and find a small helping of chopped, fresh vegetables, such as broccoli, parsley, carrots or perhaps a couple of peas. Tiny chunks of cheese, pasta or whole wheat bread, and an occasional morsel of apple or orange, can also be added to the diet.

These foods, fed sparingly, must be fresh. They should be of the same quality you would demand of your own diet. Feeding your hamster a few tiny bites of fresh food each day helps to round out the diet and to keep the hamster interested in eating. However, feeding her leftovers could result in gastric upset and obesity.

Fresh vegetables and fruits including bits of apples and oranges, lettuce, carrots, broccoli and parsley should be served to your hamster on a daily basis.

Remember that even the freshest of foods won't stay that way for long, so the uneaten portions must be removed each day to prevent spoilage. Of special concern from a sanitary standpoint is that these foods are certain to spoil if stored with a hamster's hidden supply, which is where many a hamster is apt to deliver the leftovers when mealtime is over. Keep track of what fresh foods you offer your pet, and how much you feed her. If the daily ration seems to have disappeared too quickly, search for a stash of food that will be prone to spoilage after a couple of days.

Treats should be healthful and offered to your hamster in moderation. Appropriate and highly coveted hamster treats include raisins, peanuts in the shell, a small bite of fruit and various commercially prepared treats that contain a variety of natural ingredients.

Regardless of what type of treats you choose, they must be offered sparingly so as not to interfere with the balance of the hamster's primary diet or cause gastric upset or obesity. Treats should not be viewed as an everyday event, nor should they be considered part of the basic diet. Treats can be lifesavers, particularly when a hamster escapes from her cage or disappears from where she is playing in the living room.

TREATS CAN BE LIFESAVERS

One way to find an escaped and soon-to-be-hungry hamster is to entice her out into the open by baiting each room with her favored treats. After setting traps—say, a handful of raisins in every room—the owner usually walks into a room of the house where he or she least expects to spot the hamster, and finds his or her pet sitting up on her haunches, nibbling contentedly on a raisin she holds securely in her delicate fingers.

Water occupies a most prominent spot on the list of vital nutrients and is in fact the one component that binds all the others together.

Without fresh, clean water every day, the hamster's system—or any mammal's—will be completely unable to operate. Each and every cell within the body requires water to function and to reproduce.

It is no surprise that without ample amounts of water in her system, an animal's blood cannot flow correctly, her organs cannot carry out their jobs, and her brain cannot function as it should. A lack of water (typically caused either by an empty water bottle or dish, an illness that causes her not to drink or by diarrhea) leads to dehydration, which in turn may lead to death. This can be easily prevented, of course, by supplying your small pet with fresh, clean water in squeaky clean containers every day—and monitoring how much she drinks.

How to Feed a Hamster

Once you understand the simple components of the optimum hamster diet, you must design a feeding regimen. This, not surprisingly, is just as simple as the diet itself.

The hamster is a rodent with a speedy metabolism. She must have access to food at all times to feed those ample energy needs. Although the hamster will typically eat most of her daily rations during the night, she must have food available during the day should she awaken and need a midday snack.

Hamsters are playful, avid exercisers with a very fast metabolism. Care should be taken to provide ample food during the day and especially at night, when they are most active.

FOOD DISHES

If feeding the hamster in a traditional dish, the food is best offered in a heavy ceramic bowl, weighted at the bottom to prevent her from tipping it over and leaving a mess of food and bedding on the cage floor. Nest the dish securely within the bedding of the enclosure to prevent spillage, and place it some distance from the hamster's nest box and from her designated bathroom area. In the hamster's mind, there's a distinct place for everything and everything must be in its place.

If you have a problem with the food being soiled in an open air dish situated in the middle of the enclosure— perhaps by a hamster who's favorite place to sit is inside her food dish—there are dish styles available that can clamp on to a cage wall. Such a dish must sit low enough to the floor of the habitat to make it easily accessible to the hamster.

Another option is a block-type diet administered from receptacles that hang from the enclosure wall (which must also be placed low enough for the hamster to reach). But this latter option requires the presence of an additional food dish for seed mixture if it is being offered and any fresh foods the hamster will be eating that day.

WATER CONTAINERS

Fresh water should be given each day, preferably in a water bottle mounted to the side of the enclosure with a metal sipping tube (avoid plastic tubes that can be chewed and destroyed by a hamster's gnawing). The bottle should be emptied and refilled daily with a fresh supply of water, and the sipping tube must be checked every day, too, for possible blockages that would prevent the hamster from drinking properly and getting the fluid her body needs.

You might also offer water in a heavy ceramic dish identical to the type you use for the food dish, but this is a far messier alternative and not one that is considered ideal for hamsters. Aside from the fact that the dish can become soiled with food, dust, bedding and feces as it sits exposed to the open air and the hamster's activities, there is also the danger that the water dish will spill, leaving the hamster without drinking water and a habitat floor carpeted with soaked bedding.

Check your hamster's water bottle daily to see that she is drinking enough.

77

Regardless of the equipment with which you choose to feed your hamster, all items must be cleaned thoroughly each day. Empty the previous day's contents (food or water), scrub the dish or bottle with a mild soap and warm water (avoid strong detergents and chemical disinfectants) and rinse the item thoroughly to remove all soap residues. If soap remains on the dish or bottle, the hamster could ingest it with her next meal or drink, and subsequently suffer from a nasty bout of gastric upset.

chapter 7

Keeping Your
Hamster
Healthy

As we know, our pets are not immortal. When we choose to live intimately with animals in our homes, we must acknowledge that we will outlive them. Indeed their life spans are far shorter than our own—this is especially true of hamsters that typically live only two to three years.

Although their life spans are short, we are bound by honor to do all we can to make those years as fulfilling and healthy as possible for the animals, and to alleviate any suffering they may have. There are steps we can take to help them enjoy the longest lives possible and to foster the lovely bond that can exist between an owner and his or her pet.

Preventive Care

Part of this mission is to observe the hamster for subtle changes that could indicate the early stages of a budding health problem. The medical establishment has long understood that the earlier treatment is sought for an ailment, the greater chance the patient has of recovering successfully. It is up to the animal's owner, the individual who knows the animal best, to look for those early signs. Get to know your pet's physical and behavioral characteristics when he is healthy—the texture and density of his hair; the contour of his skin and physique; the patterns of his eating, sleeping and playing behaviors; and his natural aroma—and you will be better prepared to notice any change that could indicate the first sign of a problem.

Once you are familiar with your hamster's normal behavior, you'll be able to differentiate healthy activity—like an occasional stretch—from signs of illness, like lethargy.

Warning Signs

Common Illness Some of the more common "red flag" changes to look out for are the sudden onset of uncharacteristic lethargy (especially at playtime in the late afternoon and evening); a lack of appetite; diarrhea and/or the presence of moisture around the hamster's rear end (the classic sign of the hamster ailment known as wet tail); a deterioration in the quality, density and texture of the hair (although some loss and thinning of the hair is common with age in a hamster); a swollen abdomen; incessant scratching of the skin; a failure to tend to routine grooming duties; or an unusual odor from what is essentially an odorless animal. These signs could indicate any number of conditions that require medical attention.

Acute Illness You should also be on the lookout for more complex behaviors and symptoms. A hamster that begins to exhibit circling behavior, for example, may be suffering from an ear infection. Excessive thirst and urination are serious signs that indicate kidney disease, diabetes or adrenal disease. The development of lumps or bumps under the skin could signal the presence of tumors or abscesses, which require veterinary attention. Discharge from the eye is also a cause for concern in hamsters, as they are prone to eye infections. Should such a discharge persist, contact the veterinarian for advice and/or treatment.

More veterinarians today are trained to treat small and exotic pets and encourage owners to bring pocket pets in for routine visits.

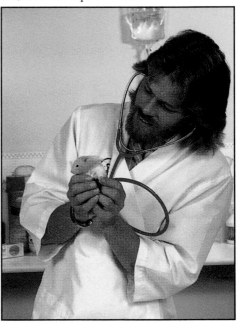

The owner who interacts daily with his or her pet hamster and observes him carefully for those telltale signs will be able to report these observations to the hamster's veterinarian early on. Early treatment and fast action will increase the opportunity for a full recovery from the illness.

PRACTICING PREVENTION

At the same time, the owner can further increase those odds—and prevent problems from beginning in the first place—by adopting responsible hamster keeping practices. For example, feed your hamster a diet of only the highest-quality ingredients in a balance that keeps fat to a minimum (keep nuts and seeds to a minimum) and that includes about 15 to 20 percent protein. This should be supplemented by fresh, clean water served in a clean water bottle with a functional sipping tube.

Your pet's housing, whether it be a glass or plastic aquarium or a wire cage, should be kept clean. Soiled bedding should be removed daily and bedding changed completely every week. A clean, dry enclosure positioned in a spot out of drafts or direct sunlight is one of the most effective tools in the keeping of a healthy hamster—and in the rehabilitation of an ailing one.

CREATING A HEALTHFUL ENVIRONMENT

Trying to alleviate your hamster's breathing difficulties by altering problem-causing agents within his environment is not only simple, but results in quick and noticeable improvement.

If, for example, you suspect cold temperatures and drafts are to blame for your hamster's noisy breathing, move your pet's enclosure to a spot that is warmer and free from drafts. If bedding dust and oils are a problem, try a pelleted paper or vegetable product and avoid cedar and wood shavings. Your hamster will breathe easier for it.

Your hamster's stress levels should also be kept at a minimum, as stress is one of the primary contributors to the deterioration of hamster health. While stress itself is not a disease-carrying agent, its presence in a hamster's life opens the door to bacteria and viruses that can harm the animal's organs and immune system. Keep stress under control by adhering to a routine in the hamster's care and to the maintenance and cleanliness of his habitat, and by restricting his interactions only to those individuals who respect the hamster and understand how to handle him correctly. Housing each hamster alone in his own roomy abode is also important in keeping stress low and preserving hamster health.

Quarantines

It is wise when bringing a new hamster into the household to quarantine him for a few weeks to ensure he doesn't bring in contagious illnesses that might infect existing pet hamsters. While the newcomer should be offered his own habitat, that habitat should be kept in a separate room during those first weeks. While it goes without saying that a new hamster, for his own safety as well as that of the other pets, should never be brought home and simply placed into an existing pet's habitat, some illnesses can be airborne, so a more formalized quarantine is necessary to ensure that all of the hamsters are healthy and present no danger to each other.

Changes with Aging

Even the most diligent adherence to preventive measures can not grant a pet hamster immortality. After his first or second birthday, you will begin to notice some changes that are common to a hamster as he ages. There may be some hair loss, some diminishment of energy levels and some subtle changes in the daily routine. The observant owner, however, will know when a change, even a minimal one, calls for medical attention.

Diseases and Conditions

ALLERGIES

Some hamsters may have allergies to certain foods and types of bedding. You may notice that your hamster is sneezing and his eyes are watery but his behavior has not changed. He may have red feet and have dry, flaky skin with some hair loss. These symptoms point to allergies, which can be treated in various ways. First, your hamster may be allergic to his food. Try feeding him a simple diet with a reduction of protein. Easily digestible foods such as white rice or white bread, fruit and vegetables and cereal (like corn flakes) are favorable. Next, try changing your hamster's bedding; he may be allergic to the filler (such as sawdust). Other causes of allergies are strong odors such as cleaning agents, cologne and cigarette smoke. Once you determine what your pet is allergic to, removal of the irritant should provide relief.

COLDS

Just like humans, hamsters are susceptible to colds and can actually catch a cold from you! A good preventive measure is to keep your hamster away from drafts and severe drops in temperature. Hamsters should be kept at a moderate room temperature.

If your hamster has symptoms such as a runny nose, watery eyes, sneezing and lethargy, he most likely has the sniffles. He will probably be curled up in a corner and may feel cool to the touch. A cold in a hamster can quickly turn into life-threatening pneumonia. Therefore he must be treated immediately by first putting his cage in a warm area that is free from drafts. An artificial light source can be put near the cage and bedding material should be abundant to provide your hamster with additional warmth. A lukewarm solution of equal parts milk and water with a teaspoon of honey should be given to your hamster. Take your hamster to the veterinarian after two days if you don't see improvement.

Daily interaction with your hamster will help you evaluate any health changes.

CONSTIPATION

Symptoms of constipation in a hamster are a distended (enlarged) belly, lethargy and arching of the back. He most likely will not want to be held or petted because of the discomfort. Lack of exercise and a decrease of wet fruit or vegetables can cause constipation. Your hamster may be so uncomfortable that he does not want to eat at all. In that case you can use an eye dropper to give him a few drops of medicinal paraffin or olive oil. The oil is usually very effective in clearing up the constipation. As your hamster is feeling better, give him plenty of wet greens (such as lettuce).

DIARRHEA

Feeding your hamster green vegetables is important, but you don't want to overfeed him or suddenly change his diet. If this happens, you will notice a very messy cage and a dirty hamster due to his loose droppings. Giving him only dry food will usually help him recover quickly. If the problem is severe, a few drops of charcoal (dissolved in water) should do the trick. You should slowly introduce green foods into the diet again, but in moderate amounts.

HEATSTROKE

Your hamster's cage should not be kept in direct sunlight or too close to a heat source because it is very easy for him to overheat. Clean, easily accessible drinking water should be available to your hamster at all times. If his fur is damp, he seems unresponsive and you can't get a wakeful reaction, speedy action must be taken. You should begin cooling your hamster by pouring cold water over him and making him drink. If he doesn't seem completely back to himself shortly, you should take him to the veterinarian right away.

WET TAIL

Perhaps the most prevalent disease in the pet hamster population is the condition known commonly as wet tail, scientifically as *proliferative ileitis*. This is a bacterial illness that causes severe diarrhea in a hamster and can, and often does, prove fatal.

All too common among newly acquired hamsters, wet tail is caused by a bacteria, but that bacteria's ability to gain a foothold in the animal's system is directly linked to conditions within the animal's environment that make his system friendly to bacterial infection.

Stress, for example, is considered an important factor in the proliferation of wet tail (and explains why the disease is so prevalent in young hamsters during their early days in new homes), as are sudden changes in

---

CLASSIC SIGNS OF WET TAIL

- watery diarrhea and, consequently, moisture around the hamster's tail

- loss of appetite

- dehydration

- unkempt hair

- rectal bleeding or rectal prolapse

- uncharacteristic irritability

A wet tail can also indicate a bladder or uterine infection or a number of other serious illnesses in hamsters. No matter what the cause, wet tail is a symptom that should be evaluated by a veterinarian immediately—the sooner the better.

Living with
Your Hamster

diet, habitat overcrowding, extreme temperatures and unsanitary living conditions.

Although wet tail is most common in young weanling hamsters, it may affect older hamsters as well, so owners should remain attuned to the symptoms—especially when new hamsters join the household. Wet tail is most often discovered in a household with new pets, the hamsters having contracted the disease at the pet shop or breeding facility from which they came. Owners are advised to watch for the telltale signs of the disease during the first few weeks of a hamster's presence in his new home. Keeping any newcomers quarantined during those first few weeks is critical as well due to the highly contagious nature of this condition.

POCKET PETS NEED VETERINARY CARE

From their own surveys on pet owners and veterinary care, the American Veterinary Medical Association has found that only about 5.02 percent of hamster owners seek veterinary care for their pets, and that's a shame. All pets, from the tiniest mouse or frog to the most expensive champion show dog, should receive necessary veterinary attention.

Hamsters have a relatively short life span, yet when we become owners we commit to all aspects of their care, including their medical care. In keeping with this philosophy, there are more veterinarians today who are experienced in caring for small and exotic animals, and more opportunities for hamster owners to seek help when their hamsters need it. Some practitioners even offer discounts to people who come to them with small animals in need of treatment.

The ultimate goal is to educate the public at large that hamsters are just as worthy of medical care as any member of the family, whether they be two-legged or four. It is acceptable, necessary and part of that grand commitment that is pet ownership.

Treatment

Treatment usually involves the administration of a combination of antibiotics, fluid therapy and antidiarrhea medications. Since medicating a hamster is a delicate task, only the veterinarian should direct such treatment. Hamsters, for example, can have severe reactions to antibiotics as well as over-the-counter remedies that promise results. It's essential that you pursue veterinary treatment at the earliest sign of a problem.

Aside from following the veterinarian's treatment regimen, keep the sick hamster away from any healthy ones in the household, and keep his habitat clean, warm and dry. A hamster's survival of wet tail is directly linked to the quality of nursing the hamster receives from his owners, and to the quality of his environment.

Preventive Antibiotics?

One controversial practice being promoted recently is the prevention of wet tail through the routine administration of antibiotics to a new hamster, whether or not he exhibits any signs of disease, just as you would vaccinate a new puppy. But because antibiotics present their own threat to hamsters, routine treatment of healthy hamsters may not only be dangerous, but also bring about an unexpected side effect. Overtreating the hamster with antibiotics without due cause and veterinary supervision may cause drug resistance. This will cause the antibiotics to be ineffective to the hamster should he require antibiotic therapy in the future for an actual illness.

Hair and Skin Problems

Hair Loss As your hamster ages, natural changes will occur in his skin and hair—a thinning or loss of hair, a thickening or blemishing of the skin, etc. Upon close examination of the hamster's daily activities, you may find that hair loss is being caused by the animal's rubbing up against rough surfaces within his enclosure. It's important to note that skin and hair changes should be closely monitored because they can indicate more serious health concerns.

If your hamster is experiencing hair loss, start by checking the cage for rough surfaces that may be causing irritation.

If, for example, hair loss is accompanied by a hamster's increased thirst, you are looking at the classic signs of adrenal disease, the treatment for which includes the surgical removal of the adrenal gland(s). Other possibilities for the cause of these symptoms include

*Always get a
veterinarian's
advice before
administering
first aid to an
injured hamster.*

thyroid disease or, in females, disease of the reproductive tract.

Parasites Hair loss and skin problems can also be caused by parasites, the most common parasites affecting hamsters being demodex mites, which cause *demodectic mange*. What's interesting about this condition is that mites are common and typically benign residents on hamsters, yet they can become a problem if the host hamster develops a more serious internal illness. That illness opens the door to a severe mite infestation, the successful treatment for which is curing the illness (then the mites). Like all serious conditions that afflict hamsters, this, too, should be presented to the veterinarian for treatment.

Abscesses Hamsters are also prone to abscesses, so the owner should also be on the lookout for lumps and bumps on the skin. The most common causes of these skin anomalies are abscesses and tumors. While abscesses, which can be quite painful if ignored, will on occasion open and drain on their own, in most cases this must be done by the veterinarian. Tumors, too, may require surgical removal depending on their type and where they are located on the hamster's body.

Scratching Hamsters are meticulously clean, but incessant, compulsive scratching is not part of the normal grooming program. The hamster driven to this may be suffering from a parasite infestation, adrenal disease, a fungal infection, liver disease, a dietary imbalance or a lack of particular nutrients. Allergies to either food or elements in the environment (such as dusty or aromatic bedding, chemical disinfectants or shampoos) can also cause abnormal scratching behavior.

INJURIES

Bleeding   Bleeding can be a sign of cancer, problems with digestive organs or a prolapsed rectum (bleeding from the rectum is especially serious in that it can indicate tumors, cancer, ulcers or intestinal problems), as well as an external injury to the hamster. This can be something as minor as a superficial cut on a leg from an exposed wire in the cage, to a foot injury from an overzealous run on the wheel, or something as severe as a bite wound from a fellow hamster that objects to sharing a habitat.

Treatment   Any type of bleeding should warrant an immediate call to the veterinarian for advice on how the hamster's particular case should be handled. He may require on-site veterinary attention to stop the bleeding or simple nursing care at home. The doctor may suggest that you administer hydrogen peroxide or betadine on a cotton swab to keep the wound clean and free of infection.

Follow the veterinarian's advice on how to deal with the wound, even with treatment as seemingly simple as the choice and application of topical antibiotic ointments or similar medications. Great care must be taken as some preparations can be absorbed into the hamster's system through the skin and prove to be toxic or even fatal. This problem may be exacerbated if the hamster licks at the wound, thus taking even more of the substance into his system.

RESPIRATORY PROBLEMS

Infections   The primary cause of breathing problems can be directly related to the respiratory system. A viral or bacterial infection, for example, may be the root of the problem. A viral infection relies on a hamster's healthy immune system to facilitate recovery; a bacterial infection may require antibiotic therapy under the direction of a veterinarian.

Environmental Causes Components within the hamster's environment may also be to blame for the animal's breathing difficulties, such as dusty or aromatic bedding materials (which can also harm the animal's liver), cold drafts that infiltrate the hamster's habitat or allergens or chemical fumes in the hamster's atmosphere.

Some hamsters experience respiratory problems due to bedding dust.

Underlying Problems Difficulty breathing may signal a more severe internal illness, such as a heart problem, that breaks down the respiratory system. Respiratory problems caused by an underlying, and typically even more serious, health condition can be corrected only by addressing that primary condition first. The veterinarian must be contacted immediately at the onset of respiratory symptoms, as this is the person best equipped to determine what is the root of respiratory distress in your hamster.

Unexpected Pregnancy

As we have seen, there is no shortage of hamsters on the pet market. Unfortunately, good permanent homes for the many hamsters bred and born each year are not abundant. In light of this situation, intentionally breeding your hamster, unless you intend to keep all of the offspring you produce for the duration of their lives, is not a particularly responsible avenue to pursue.

Some people believe they can make money from breeding hamsters. Another motivation for breeding among pet owners is the assumption that this is the ideal way to teach the kids "the miracle of life." Again, these ideas fail to take into account the well-being of the hamsters and the often insurmountable challenge of finding good, permanent homes for them—thus imparting an additional, much sadder, lesson to the children about pet overpopulation and homelessness. When entertaining the idea of breeding, pet owners are wise to remind themselves that they bought this animal for companionship. They brought him into their home for the opportunity to coexist with a species so different from their own, to revel in how blessed we humans are to be able to adopt such creatures and live happily in their presence. In most cases, breeding is best kept out of the equation.

Unfortunately, sometimes accidents happen. With hamsters this often occurs at the beginning of the owner/hamster relationship with an owner who has no intention of breeding his or her pets. This individual discovers several weeks after bringing a pair of allegedly female hamsters home, that those two hamsters have become a family of seven, eight, maybe nine. Such owners will need a crash course in the care of that new little family, both to help them survive and to prevent a repeat performance in the future.

BREEDING BASICS

Hamsters boast one of the quickest reproduction rates in the animal kingdom. Reaching sexual maturity at about two months of age, hamster gestation is also phenomenally short—about sixteen days. No wonder the hamster isn't anywhere near the threat of extinction.

When kept in captivity as pets, hamsters are sometimes housed together, but instinctively they prefer a solitary existence. The classic wild hamster, however, would typically come together with other hamsters only for breeding, after which they would go their separate ways, leaving the female to raise her young as a single mother.

It's best not to interfere while the hamster prepares a nest for her litter.

Hamster breeders today tend to follow this same natural pattern: housing the hamsters separately, placing a female in estrus with the designated male only at the opportune time. Even then, the caretaker must watch the pair carefully. A female who doesn't happen to be in the mood can be dangerous to the amorous male in her midst. Therefore, if she isn't ready, it's best to keep the two apart until she is (and to remove the male after a successful mating has taken place).

About two weeks later, the female will be ready to give birth. Before this occurs, the owner should clean her enclosure and replace the bedding with a thick layer of clean shavings, for she will have to remain undisturbed with her young for the first couple of weeks after they are born.

As her due date approaches, the mother-to-be will become restless. This is the signal that her owner should refrain from handling and playing with her. A day or two later, as if by magic, the owner will probably just happen to notice that suddenly the enclosure is occupied by the new mom and a litter of five to ten naked babies.

CARE OF THE LITTER

Hamster mothers don't appreciate interference from humans, so the little family is best left alone for a week or two to prevent stress. If the mother feels stressed or threatened during those first couple of weeks, she may destroy her young. It is best to resist the temptation to get involved and let nature take its course.

As the weeks pass, the young hamsters will sprout hair, begin to share their mother's solid food (although they will not be completely weaned until they are almost a month old) and begin to venture farther away from Mom's side. Before you know it, they too will look at the world with that cheeky, whimsical expression that sets the hamster apart from all other rodents and has made the hamster famous.

The owner of these hamsters is then faced with the challenge of placing the young animals into new and permanent homes. While siblings can usually coexist for a while, you may have to separate them if placing them takes longer than you intended. And indeed that is the hard part. The breeding is easy, the responsibility of placement is tough and not something the unsuspecting new owner—the accidental breeder—ever expects to have to deal with.

When faced with this responsibility, your best option is to contact the local animal shelter(s). Whether or not they are adopting hamsters themselves, you can ask them to refer people looking for hamster pets to you. You will need to screen potential owners who are interested in adopting. You should ask about their families, other pets, living situation, hamster knowledge, etc. Gauge their commitment to this little pet and be sure they are serious about the responsibility.

Remember that releasing pet animals into the wild is not only cruel, it also wreaks havoc with native wildlife by interfering with their food chain and natural habitat. If you come to the point where you simply cannot find proper homes for the hamsters or keep them yourself, euthanasia may be the only alternative, performed either at the animal shelter or by your own veterinarian.

This is unfortunate but far more humane and responsible than seeing hamsters go to inappropriate homes, or releasing them into the wild to face starvation, injury, illness and countless other dangers for which they are not prepared. When all is said and done, share your experiences with other new owners. Education about the pitfalls of breeding will do them and their pets a favor, as well as the hamster species as a whole.

When It's Time

Loving your hamster is an emotional investment with wonderful rewards. Unfortunately, there comes a time when you have to say good-bye to a pet. One of the kindest things you can do for a hamster who is severely injured or extremely ill and suffering is to have your veterinarian end his pain peacefully and humanely through euthanization.

Euthanasia is a painless injection that induces death quickly. After a relaxing tranquilizer, your veterinarian will give your pet the injection that will immediately put the animal into a deep and quiet unconsciousness that leads to death.

Deciding to euthanize your pet is very difficult but sometimes necessary for the well-being of your pet and your family. Ultimately your decision is a personal one, but can be aided by friends and family. Your veterinarian will also be able to help you determine your pet's quality of life and will support your choice. Since your veterinarian can't make your decision, make sure you completely understand your pet's diagnosis and general health. Take some time to think through your decision.

SAYING GOOD-BYE

Being honest about your emotions is the best way to start coping with the loss of your pet. The act of saying good-bye will help you express your grief. Since you are losing an important part of your life, it is normal to feel sad and experience feelings of loss. Once you have decided to euthanize your pet, you may want to plan a special time for you and your family members to be alone with your pet and say a private good-bye.

After you have lost your pet, allow yourself time to grieve and accept that you will need a while to adjust to your life without your hamster. Talk to friends and relatives and remember that talking about your loss will often help in the healing process. You will always have loving memories of the happy times you shared with your pet.

Enjoying
Your

part three

Hamster

chapter 8

Understanding

Your

Hamster

Imagine that you are just 5 inches long, stand only 2 inches tall and weigh only a few ounces.

Imagine, too, that your natural instincts tell you, the diminutive critter that you are, that you should sleep by day safely hidden in solitude within tunnels beneath the ground, and awaken in the evening to hunt for food under the cover of darkness.

Yet despite these powerful callings, you find yourself in a household of odd two-legged creatures who tower above you; who hoist you into the air, away from the safety of your beloved terra firma, often waking you from your peaceful day's slumber to do so. Even though you prefer living alone, you may have to coexist with another hamster and share your enclosure as well as your food.

A Hamster's Perspective

Think about it. This is how we must look to the hamsters in our lives—and how they must perceive humans. Viewed in this light, our world must be a pretty scary place for these tiny animals.

But our world need not, nor should it be, a frightening place for the hamster. In the right caretaker's hands, hamsters can be amazingly adaptable little creatures. We can use this characteristic to our mutual benefit: to make life more pleasant for the hamster and to make her care as simple as possible for us.

The first step in this noble mission is to take the time to learn all that you can about this unique little creature, and then to make the effort to see our world through her eyes. Through this fascinating, educational journey, you will learn that the hamster is more than willing to work with her owners in forging the unique bond that can result in a mutually satisfying relationship between owner and pocket pet.

In getting to know the hamster, you will also learn—we would hope not by experience, of course—that stress can take a profound physical and emotional toll on this tiny animal. Seeing the world through your hamster's eyes is the first step toward preventing stress in your pet's life. The hamster who comes into the care of an individual who has made this effort is a lucky hamster indeed.

A compassionate owner is able to look at the world from the hamster's perspective.

Hamster Highlights

Cheeks Hamsters are famous for their puffy cheek pouches. The holding capacity of the pockets is such that they double the size of the hamster's head when filled completely! They enable the hamster to stow away food that is not eaten immediately. When the hamster returns to her home she empties her pouches by stroking her paws along her cheeks. The cheek pouches are also a defense technique—when a hamster feels threatened she puffs up her pouches to make herself appear larger.

Teeth Like all rodents, hamsters have ever-growing incisors. The incisors continue to grow because they have no roots. It is necessary that hamsters do a lot of gnawing; the continual chewing keeps the incisors sharp and at a manageable length. Hamsters have very strong teeth and muscles associated with chewing.

Legs How do they have the strength for all that running? Hamsters have muscular front legs with paws used for burrowing, climbing and getting themselves out of precarious positions. Their back legs are for support and aren't quite as strong as their front legs.

Eyes Like many animals that are more active at night, hamsters have big eyes that seem to pop out at you. Their vision isn't perfect because they are far-sighted. They are able to spot other animals in time to protect themselves due to the fact that their eyes are positioned laterally (giving them a greater angle of vision).

Ears Your hamster can tell the difference between you and her other caretakers because her hearing is extremely sensitive. The hearing is so well developed that she can probably hear sounds in extremely high frequencies. If you see your hamster flinch, she may have heard something that you were not able to pick up.

Smell The world of the hamster is defined by her acute sense of smell. She can establish her living environment, who her caretakers and enemies are, and when another hamster is sexually mature. Hamsters recognize each other by distinct scents (secreted by glands) that become familiar by grooming and nesting together. If hamsters are separated temporarily or placed in completely different living quarters, it is very difficult to have hamsters peacefully coexist again because the scent has changed.

Touch   Whiskers, or vibrissa, are the main organ that hamsters use to investigate their environment. Spatial sense and ability to detect objects blocking her way are determined by your hamster's whiskers.

WILL THE REAL HAMSTER PLEASE STAND UP?

Most people you meet assume they understand hamsters. What's to understand? They are quiet little rodents without a care in the world who eat, sleep and sometimes run on a wheel. There's not much more to them, is there? If you look at the misconceptions that people have about hamsters, you may be surprised by what you'll learn about the true hamster personality.

Misconception   Hamsters are easy-care pets and don't require much interaction with their owners.

Fact   Hamsters do require attention from their owners. They thrive on it. And this must be provided on a regular routine basis, not just when the owner removes the hamster from her cage once a week for her routine cleaning. Though hamsters are not crazy about others of their own kind, they, for some reason, tend to enjoy the company of humans. This bond, however, takes time to develop and is not something that can be forced from your hamster.

Your hamster will thrive on lots of consistent love and affection from you—the more the better.

Misconception   Hamsters are annoying; all they do is run endlessly on their wheels all night, keeping everyone awake with the wheel's squeaking.

Fact   Those who know and work with hamsters, whether they be pet owners, veterinarians or animal welfare activists, know that far too many hamsters are lonely hamsters left in their cages with little or nothing to do. Hamsters can't bark like dogs to alert their owners to their loneliness. They don't chew up shoes or destroy furniture in blatant exhibitions of frustration. They have no choice but to languish within their cages, sleeping even more than they would like to, perhaps eating more than they need to and running endlessly on a squeaky wheel that is their only outlet for exercise.

The hamster would prefer to eat, sleep, burrow into the bedding of her enclosure, play with a variety of toys and, yes, spend a bit of time each day interacting with her owners.

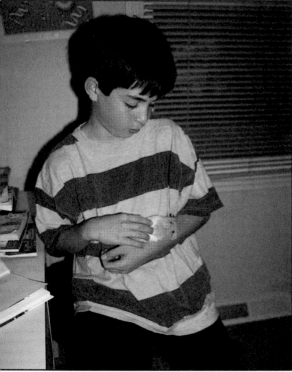

Gradually intro-ducing your ham-ster to new people when she is young will result in a more trusting pet.

Misconception Hamsters are nasty, difficult to socialize and are prone to biting.

Fact Depending on your pet's personality, with proper, gradual and gentle handling, she may choose to trust and respond to you and perhaps one or two other people, or she may take a more openly social approach and embrace all humans who enter her realm. Either way, respect the animal for what she is most comfortable with. The hamster in turn will respect you and reward you with her own brand of hamster affection. Socialize your hamster gently and gradually to a variety of people and experiences at an early age. Establish a set routine for your pet, allow her to nap peacefully and undisturbed during the day, protect her from rough handling, loud voices and sounds and household dangers.

Hamsters and Other Pets

While socialization, especially at a young age, is an important element to the upbringing of the healthy, well-adjusted hamster, this is best limited only to the humans in the hamster's household and their human friends and relatives. While we may enjoy envisioning all pets coexist and interact happily with one another, from the dog and cat all the way to the tiny hamster, fostering such a scene with the hamster is not a good idea.

Yes, you may have seen a photograph of a large dog resting peacefully alongside an inquisitive hamster. But such a scene will only stress the hamster—a tiny prey animal, after all—that is forced to interface unprotected with a large predator. An animal lover who shares his or her home with a variety of species is wise to respect each of those animals: not to tease the cat by dangling a delectable hamster in its face, or to stress that hamster by presenting her to the resident predator. The hamster will live just as happily—and probably longer—if she never interacts with other family pets. The only family member she needs is you.

Beware! Any opening, large or small, is ample temptation for your hamster to make a run for freedom.

The Escape Artist

Hamsters are consummate escape artists. Far too many hamster owners learn this the hard way. When owners compare hamster stories, you're likely to hear fantastic tales of hamster escapes and, hopefully, lost hamster recoveries. Understand this animal's propensity to run, take it seriously, and you can prevent your hamster from getting lost.

The escapes usually occur because of human error. The cage door is left open; the hamster is allowed to run unsupervised through the house; the hamster is housed in a wooden enclosure that proves no match to the animal's gnawing abilities; or perhaps a child is left to care for the animal when he or she is either too young for such a responsibility or uninterested in expending the necessary energy.

Sometimes the hamster takes advantage of a situation and creates her own escape route—and writes her own story. She discovers a hole in the screen wall of her enclosure and works diligently to enlarge that hole to accommodate her own small frame. She discovers the latch is broken on the door of her cage and works all night long to spring it. She chews through the plastic walls of her tube habitat. Or, during a foray outside of her cage, she discovers an open door to the wilderness or a heating grate on the floor and cannot deny the calling to follow her insatiable curiosity down the rabbit hole, so to speak.

> ## AMAZING ESCAPES
>
> Many lost hamsters have been known to show up in the most unexpected, even shocking, places: in toilets, in sinks, in outdoor trash cans, beneath the cushions of the living room furniture (quite dangerous if those are cushions of a reclining chair), in household furnaces or in kitchen pantries. Lose a hamster and be prepared to find her anywhere!
>
> Stories abound of hamsters popping up, even up to a year following their disappearance, perhaps stealing sunflower seeds from the birdhouse; nonchalantly nibbling greenery in the vegetable garden; or exploring the folds and wrinkles of the sheets of her owner's bed.
>
> The owner is always amazed at how the hamster is able to sustain herself with food and water during her absence, and never loses sight of the fact that the animal's reappearance is nothing short of a miracle.

Survival Outdoors

When a hamster thought lost and gone forever is rediscovered, her owner may wonder how she was able to steer clear of the resident cats or other such predators. This is especially true of the hamster that escapes into the great outdoors. Countless threats await this tiny animal that has no experience surviving in our domestic neighborhoods. Yet survive many do, and while this is good for the hamster, it has broader repercussions to other wildlife within that ecosystem.

The hamster, the golden hamster in particular, is a desert native, one that has not evolved among the various species that we most often encounter in the typical western hemisphere neighborhood. Her introduction to such an area will throw the natural ecosystem off kilter, disturbing the balance of nature and the food chain within that area.

A single lost hamster will probably cause little harm, but it's a different story if several people in a given area decide they no longer want their pets and set them free in the wild. Aside from the ecological problems this can cause, setting this tiny animal free to fend for herself is downright cruel. If for any reason you can no longer keep your pet, the kindest way to deal with this quandary is to personally find her a new home or take her to the animal shelter.

PREVENTING ESCAPE

Take great care to monitor your pet carefully at all times, when she is in her enclosure and when she is out and about playing. Examine the cage regularly for holes, gaps or loose latches—anything the hamster may eventually use to escape—and immediately make the necessary repairs or change the habitat. Whenever your hamster is out of her cage, supervise her carefully and make sure she has no access to open doors or any such escape routes. By the same token, never leave your hamster in the care of someone who is not as diligent in your pet's supervision as you are.

HAMSTER HIDEOUTS

Did you turn your back for a moment and your pet made a run for it? Look in dark spots; check your stacks of magazines and newspapers; check inside sofa cushions, mattresses and boxes of any sort. Listen for scuffling or scratching sounds nearby. Hamsters love to burrow, so chances are she is dozing in a cozy self-made nest.

Special Circumstances

Once you master the basics of hamster care and get to know your individual pet, you should encounter few problems in your relationship with this unique and enchanting animal. But circumstances may arise that test the routine you have established in caring for your pocket pet—circumstances to which you will both need to adjust.

During the winter it is important to keep your hamster in a warm environment, between 65 and 80 degrees Fahrenheit, to avoid dormancy.

DORMANCY

Imagine that an unexpected, unseasonal cold snap hits your area—so cold that the temperature within your home takes a severe dip or perhaps causes your power to go out for a couple of days. In the midst of this you notice your hamster slowing down, sleeping more and playing less.

Your hamster probably isn't ill. Rather, the cold temperatures are triggering the dormancy mechanism in her system. If left unchecked, the hamster will not hibernate in the classic sense, but she will eventually drift into a dormant sleep, a type of hibernation from which she can awake easily with a warming of the atmospheric temperature.

It's not a good idea to allow your hamster to drift into this state. The animal may not be healthy enough to withstand this process physically, and it just isn't wise to keep this animal in temperatures lower than 65 degrees Fahrenheit. This is an indoor pet, pure and simple. If you notice that she is succumbing to a dormant state, gradually warm up her environment (in a safe way, of course, without direct heat or sunlight), and make sure she enjoys the winter wide awake and alert.

GOING ON VACATION?

There comes a time in all our lives when we must travel and leave our pets behind. Here, too, the hamster shines as an easy-care pet.

A hamster can be left alone for a weekend—a three-day weekend maximum, as long

Entrust your hamster to a responsible person when you vacation.

as you leave her with all the comforts she will require. Leave her an ample helping of food (more than you would feed for a single day), and make sure you leave only foods that won't spoil while you are gone. Water is also an important staple. To be safe, leave two bottles of fresh water rather than just one, just in case one of the sipping tubes becomes clogged while you are away. Clean the enclosure and change the bedding, make sure the premises are secure, check the latches and locks of the hamster's enclosure, leave your pet a couple of her safest toys, and you're in business.

If you will be gone longer than two or three days, you need to make more detailed arrangements. You may want to ask a friend or neighbor to come in and clean the bedding, feed the hamster and change the water, or contract with a pet sitter to care for your pet. If these options are not possible, you may even be able to take your pet to a boarding kennel. Pet hotels as well as veterinary boarding facilities frequently welcome small pets as well as dogs and cats.

ON THE ROAD

Don't discount the possibility of taking your pet with you, either. These small, quiet, odorless pets can make wonderful traveling companions, assuming they are well-adjusted and comfortable with their owners. The key word here, however, is "well-adjusted." Timid, easily frightened animals will find travel stressful, and stress, in turn, can lead to a variety of health and behavior problems.

If you do deem your hamster to be a good travel candidate and decide to take her with you, bring along a secure, escape-proof cage (one of the plastic carrying-case type models would be ideal) as your pet's home away from home. Bring plenty of food, fresh bedding and toys, and you should find hamster care on the road to be a breeze. Just remind yourself that you must be even more diligent in your supervision of your pet than you are at home. When you arrive at your destination, don't allow strange people or animals to traumatize or stress your pet. Keep to your normal routine, allow your hamster her daytime naps, and you should

> ### CREATURE COMFORTS
>
> There are certain necessities your hamster will need if you plan to leave her alone for a weekend (three days maximum). Supply a generous helping of food that won't spoil (more than for a single day). Leave at least two bottles of fresh water just in case one of the sipping tubes becomes clogged while you're away. A clean cage and fresh bedding are important, as well as securely fastened latches and locks in the hamster's cage. Don't forget to provide a couple of her favorite toys or tell her that you'll be back soon.

all enjoy a pleasant trip that will be remembered fondly.

Hamster Smarts

Despite the fact that hamsters act mainly on instinct, they are also very inquisitive and intelligent. Their behavior patterns are intrinsic, yet they have the ability to retain new information through repetition. Hamsters have the ability to distinguish between caretaker and stranger due to their acute sense of smell and ablility to recognize voices. They also have a good memory for finding past food opportunities; hamsters often return to places where they had been given a treat several days before. Hamsters are incredibly creative when it comes to obtaining and transporting food to a cache.

Did You See That?

One of the most enjoyable aspects of owning a hamster is the time you take playing with her and observing her in her daily routine. You will notice that hamsters have many unique expressions and activities, one of which is grooming. When a hamster spends a lot of time washing her face and ears it means that she feels at home and is comfortable in her environment. You can also tell your hamster is relaxed when you see her stretching. At times you may observe your hamster popping into the air, expressing her happy spirit in a burst of energy.

When a hamster feels nervous or suspects danger, she may sit up on her haunches and sniff the air for a short time. If she starts walking with rigid legs and her tail sticking straight up, it means that she is fearful of something. A reaction to a loud or abrupt noise may sometimes cause your hamster to suddenly start grooming for an extended time. Grooming helps the hamster focus on herself—this is a helpful distraction from feeling fearful. Her ears will also most likely be folded back as she attempts to discern the noise that startled her.

Most vocalizations made by hamsters are to express aggression. When hamsters attack each other you may hear the aggressor growling, hissing, chattering teeth or making a muttering sound. The hamster in a defensive posture may screech to express fear.

One of the great aspects of pet ownership is the unique relationship you create with your pet. The more time you spend with your hamster, the more you will understand her behaviors and activity patterns. Hamsters learn to recognize and respond to your smell and tone of voice. When you come into the room your pet may even greet you for some playtime outside of her cage.

chapter 9

Fun

with Your

Hamster

As seasoned and dedicated hamster owners know, hamsters just want to have fun. These animals, evolved to travel several miles a night in search of food and, therefore, have a great deal of energy to expend. In the absence of vast deserts or similar wild territories to traverse as part of the hamster's daily routine, toys and games are the ideal instruments for helping captive hamsters expend that energy for optimum health and longevity.

As an energetic hamster's owner, it's your job to make sure he pursues this grand mission as safely as possible. What an honor it is to know that the hamster, a species so dramatically different from our own, chooses humans above his fellow hamsters as his playmates.

And how comforting to know that living up to that responsibility is relatively simple and fun.

Fun with Toys

Hamster fun and games revolve around toys. Contrary to popular belief, hamsters need far more than a wheel to keep themselves well-rounded and properly exercised. They thrive best with a variety of toys and games, all of which require the personal involvement of their owners. Manage the toys as you would the toys of a small child: Keep them in good repair and rotate them daily so that the hamster never has the opportunity to take his toys for granted. Then sit back and enjoy watching the animal rejoice when you reintroduce toys that have been hidden away for a few days.

THE WHEEL

It's important to rotate in other toys to avoid overuse of the exercise wheel.

While the wheel's use can be abused, it's not necessary to deprive a hamster of this classic toy. But it should not be offered as the hamster's sole toy, nor should it be offered for hours and hours at a time.

A hamster that keeps his family up at night because he spends his entire night running on a wheel is a hamster that is not receiving the optimum care he deserves. By all means allow the hamster to partake of this favored hamster activity, but allowing him to do so endlessly will result in an exhausted, and possibly dehydrated, pet.

Restricting the hamster's access to the wheel means placing the wheel within his habitat only when you wish the hamster to play with it. In other words, don't leave it in the enclosure permanently—offer other diversions to occupy his time. Periodic, sporadic use will not only help to maintain the hamster's health, but also enhance the activity for the hamster because it's not a constant in the animal's daily life. You may enhance the wheel for yourself by greasing it with petroleum jelly to keep the squeak under control.

Hamsters have an abundance of energy and love to exercise by running in a ball.

When choosing a wheel for your hamster, make sure it's the right size for your particular pet. A dwarf hamster, for example, requires a wheel smaller than one appropriate for its larger golden cousin. Once you have chosen the appropriate wheel, keep it in good working order, spinning smoothly and free of exposed hardware and sharp edges. Finally, take care to fill the remainder of your pet's playtime hours with other toys, as well, offering him a broad spectrum of activities that will keep him healthy in both mind and body.

THE BALL

Another item that has become a favorite among hamsters and their owners alike is the so-called hamster ball. This is a plastic ball into which the hamster is placed so he can run as he would on the wheel. But instead of remaining in one place, the hamster "rolls" the ball through the house fully protected by the plastic shell that surrounds him.

The balls come in a variety of sizes: smaller ones for dwarf hamsters, larger ones for goldens (placing a dwarf in a ball designed for a larger animal can be dangerous to the diminutive creature, so choose accordingly). They provide the hamster with safe, self-propelled vehicles for exploring the household. The balls may also be placed on specially designed tracks if you prefer that your pet remains confined to one specific area.

TOY SAFETY TIPS

- Only give toys composed of materials that are nontoxic

- Toys should be structurally safe; no rough edges or loose parts

- Check toys frequently for damage that could injure the hamster

- Don't give your pet toys with small pieces that could break off and be swallowed

Hamster balls provide a great deal of entertainment to a hamster, and can become an unexpected source of fascination and conversation for the hamster's owner. Owners tell, for instance, of hamsters that become so proficient in navigating these mobile toys that they chase resident cats through the hallways.

Get creative with the types of diversions you give your hamster, but don't forget safety.

But the hamster ball, too, can be abused. As with the wheel, to allow a hamster to overdo it with the ball is to invite exhaustion and dehydration, neither of which this tiny animal is well-equipped to tolerate. If you restrict the hamster's usage of the ball, keep it in good repair and supervise the animal, the ball can prove to be a productive, healthy toy that is as much fun for the hamster to use as it is for the owner to watch.

OTHER TOYS

The world can be the hamster's oyster with a steady stream of toys reintroduced intermittently every few days to maintain the hamster's interest.

The items within a hamster toy box can be a variety of commercially available toys designed especially for hamster play.

Remember that the commercial tube housing configuration can also make a wonderful playground, even if you prefer housing your pet in a more traditional cage or tank habitat. Many owners have found that hamsters

tend to gnaw through the plastic of such housing or have deemed the tubes too complicated to clean regularly. However, the tube setup can offer a hamster the ideal environment for exercise and mental stimulation outside of his home enclosure.

Use your imagination. You never know what might become a hamster's favorite toy, but in evaluating potential candidates, keep safety foremost in your mind. Both structure and material are significant when one is making, evaluating and purchasing hamster toys. This applies throughout each toy's life, during which time you must check it periodically for damage that could prove dangerous to your hamster. Make sure your hamster's toys are composed of materials that are nontoxic, structurally safe and cannot be easily destroyed by gnawing. Also check to see that toys aren't riddled with small pieces that can break off and be swallowed.

Hamsters enjoy playing in tubes, such as this commercial type, because they simulate the tunnels of the hamster's natural environment.

HOMEMADE TOYS FOR HAMSTERS

A great way to save money and get creative is to make toys at home for your hamster. Keep in mind that nothing should have sharp edges or toxic substances. You never want to use things that could suffocate your pet—like a plastic bag—to construct a toy. Remember that hamsters love to burrow, nest and use their boundless energy when playing. The following are some things you can use to make your own toys:

- Paper bags
- Shoe boxes
- PVC tubes
- Toilet paper rolls
- Wrapping paper rolls
- Old slippers

Now that you have the supplies, it is time to get imaginative! Hamsters love to exercise and explore their surroundings. You can satisfy this need by making mazes out of empty cardboard rolls/boxes. Use nontoxic glue to connect the ends of the rolls/boxes to each other. Be sure to make the toy wide enough for your hamster to fit through comfortably.

Interesting exploration outside of the cage is an important part of keeping your hamster mentally stimulated.

Since hamsters love to burrow, old slippers and socks make for great fun. Your hamster may take the stuffing out of your slippers to nest with or may simply take a nap inside a slipper. Socks may also be taken apart to nest with but also make an interesting place to burrow.

Another great toy for climbing and hiding can be made of facial tissue boxes with various-size holes cut into the sides. You can glue the boxes together and stack them on top of each other or place them side by side. The possibilities are many and, keeping safety in mind at all times, are a great way for you to get creative and also get your kids involved in the fun of pet ownership.

Out and About

As much as hamsters enjoy playing with various toys within the secure confines of their enclosures, they also relish the opportunity to leave their happy homes from time to time and explore the world beyond the cage door.

Needless to say, granting this wish can be dangerous if certain tenets of safety and decorum are not met each and every time the hamster is allowed to roam. First, the room in which the hamster will be must be made hamster-safe before the animal is allowed out to explore. For example, floor heating vents must be covered; all doors and windows out of the room must be closed; pet dogs, cats and other animals should be safely confined in another room; those delectable electrical cords must be safely moved out of the hamster's line of vision and access; and virtually anything that might attract the attention of this inquisitive animal and cause him harm should be removed. One mistake, a one-time deviation from these rules of conduct, and your pet hamster could be gone forever.

An even safer option is to establish a play area for the hamster outside of his habitat—a playpen, if you will—in which he can enjoy playing beyond the walls of his home enclosure while still enjoying the same level of safety. As we have seen, the plastic tube housing setup provides such a play area, but you can also build a makeshift enclosure with temporary wall boundaries—perhaps a child's wading pool or a large plastic storage box.

Furnish the playpen with your pet's favorite toys and sit back and enjoy as he explores his new environment, the new sights and sounds and the new objects in his path. When you establish a play area, however, you must not leave the hamster unsupervised; he must be supervised at all times during his forays away from home. Never underestimate the hamster's escape abilities, which will be even more effective in this low-security, temporary enclosure.

Sharing the Joy of Hamsters

Caring for your hamster generally proves to be a private pursuit once you find yourself enamored with this delightful pet. However, there are opportunities that link hamster owners together so they can share their mutual affections for and fascinations with these animals. Meeting others who share your passions makes hamster keeping all the more enjoyable.

For show-and-tell, the young owner can explain to fellow classmates hamster nutrition and housing, as well as how to hold the pet.

SHOW-AND-TELL

Because hamsters are often members of households where children reside, it's inevitable that one day one of the kids will want to take the family's pet hamster to school for show-and-tell. This provides not only a unique and, we would hope pleasant, outing for the animal (leave the more timid animal at home), but it also provides the child with the opportunity to educate his or her peers on proper hamster keeping.

Taking the family pet to school for all of his or her classmates to admire can make a child so proud. It's best that this foray be supervised by a parent, of course, (or at least a teacher well-versed in hamster care) to prevent accidents, escapes or similar tragedies. For the hamster's safety, he should not be passed around to everyone in the class.

As the members of the class ooh and ahh over the lovely, sweet-faced pocket pet, his young owner can tell them all about the nutrition, attention, housing and health care required to keep a hamster healthy and as long-lived as possible. As an added bonus, perhaps the other kids will take some of the inform-ation home to their own families and to their own hamsters. It's a sit-uation where everyone wins and all because a child wishes to share his or her love for hamsters.

THE HAMSTER SHOW

You have no doubt heard of dog shows, horse shows and cat shows, but believe it or not, hamsters may be exhibited in the formal show environment, as well. Surpris-ingly, these shows aren't necessar-ily all that different from those that showcase larger animals.

Typically sponsored by local and national hamster clubs, shows may be held as individual events, or they may be incorporated into other similar exhibitions, such as rat and mouse shows, county fairs or pet shows that showcase all species of companion animals. They are run very much as shows for other species, with specified classes for the entrants (in this case, classes for the different coat and color varieties). The winners of these classes then typically move up to com-pete with increasingly smaller groups of entrants until one hamster is finally proclaimed Best in Show.

Who knows? Your winsome pet could take home a prize in a local hamster show.

The hamsters are usually displayed anonymously in show cages, the cage styles designated by the club sponsoring the show to promote fairness. The ham-sters within those cages are judged on their color, structure, hair quality and temperament.

Show hamsters are not usually average pet hamsters—unless the show includes pet classes. The more tradtional show hamsters tend to be the products of dedicated breeders who have added breeding and showing to their list of enjoyable hamster pursuits. They become so enamored of their pets that they seek to show them off to others who share a passion for hamsters.

Such individuals are those that fledgling and would-be exhibitors should seek to meet. The veterans are in turn wise to welcome newcomers to the fold and to share with them their knowledge and perhaps even representatives of their show stock. Only by bringing new blood—and new hamsters—into the realm of hamster showing will the activity have a chance of surviving into future generations.

HAMSTER STANDARDS

So you're thinking that you have a prize-winning hamster and you're not sure how he measures up. The following are guidelines for Syrian hamster exhibition as determined by the British Hamster Association in 1992. American clubs may use variations on this standard.

Type (25 points) The body shall be broad and cobby. The head shall be large in proportion to the body, with a broad skull, short face and blunt nose. The head shall be well set into the body, the profile showing a smooth curve from nose over head, to nape of neck.

Fur (20 points) The fur shall be soft and very dense. Special attention shall be paid to the density of the belly fur. In short haired hamsters the fur shall be very short and even. In long haired hamsters allowance must be made for sex, i.e., males must have longer fur than females. Matting will be heavily penalised.

Size (10 points) The hamster shall be as large as possible but not too fat. Allowance shall be made for sex, i.e., female hamsters are, in general, larger than males.

Condition (10 points)   The hamster shall be fit, alert when well awake, and tame and handleable. The flesh shall be firm with no surplus fat. The coat shall have a healthy sheen, and the hamster shall be clean and show no obvious sign of injury.

Eyes and Ears (5 points)   The eyes shall be large, prominent and widely set. The ears shall be whole, large, rounded, set well apart and carried erect and unfolded when the hamster is awake.

Colour and Markings (30 points)   Eye colour: The following sequence of eye colours shall apply in increasing order of darkness:

1. Bright pink
2. Red
3. Claret red
4. Claret
5. Ruby
6. Garnet
7. Black

For patterned hamsters, 15 points shall be allocated for colour and markings and 15 points for pattern.

Where base colour is indicated, this applies to the whole animal.

Coat Types   The *rex* coat is thick, soft and frizzy all over. The *satin* coat is similar to the rex coat in density but is has a glossy shine. *Long haired* hamsters have soft, dense fur that is long all over the body except for the face.

Colour Varieties   The various **agouti** (mottled fur) varieties include beige, blonde, cinnamon, dark golden (wild type agouti), light golden (wild type agouti), dark gray, light gray, honey, lilac, rust (also known as guinea gold), smoke pearl, yellow and ivory.

Self (one colour) varieties include sable, copper, black eyed cream, red eyed cream, red eyed ivory, dark eared white/albino, flesh eared white/albino.

Among the **patterned** varieties are the *dominant spot* (white hamster with colored spots), *white banded* (colored hamster with a white band superimposed), and *tortoiseshell and white* (three color pattern; colored, yellow and white patches).

On the Internet

In this day and age of an ever-burgeoning maze of Internet web sites and on-line services, hamster owners are being offered another, rather high-tech, method for getting to know other hamster lovers all over the world. Little by little, hamster owners are developing a vast hamster network on the computer. This network includes bulletin boards, veterinary advice forums and information on everything from the nuances of hamster care to special problems to behavior to breeding. The list goes on and on, as does the potential for this relatively newfound phenomenon that can bring together hamster enthusiasts from all countries and walks of life.

As these followers go on-line, sharing their experiences in this rather contemporary way, the object of their efforts—the pet hamster—is destined to benefit. Highlighted as part of the Internet revolution, the hamster cannot help but find an important and lasting niche, one in which his care can only continue to improve in the twenty-first century.

Hamster Bytes

Go on-line for resources and to share the experience of hamster ownership.

- **Go Pets: CompuServe**   A computer forum of information on exotic and small pets. Available to subscribers of CompuServe.

- **The Pet Care Forum: America Online**   A computer forum providing information on all pet species; including thorough coverage of hamsters (veterinary advice, basic care, message boards, etc.) Available to AOL subscribers.

Here are some useful web sites that have educational information on hamsters—including facts on care, showing your pet, behavioral information and fun things you can do with your hamster.

alt.pets.hamsters: News Server

A hamster-related news group where you can chat on-line with other hamster owners. This is a great way to learn up-to-the-minute information about hamsters.

alt.pets.hamsters FAQ:
URL: http://www.jagnet.demon.com.uk/hamster/faq.html

This is a maintained document listing the Frequently Asked Questions for the alt.pets.hamsters news group.

Electronic Zoo/NetVet—Rodent Page:
URL: http://netvet.wustl.edu/rodents.htm

A comprehensive database of veterinary resources.

HandiLinks To Animals—Hamsters:
URL: http://www.ahandyguide.com/cat1/a/a695.htm

This page has pictures of hamsters, general guidelines for care and information on clubs and shows.

The Hamster Page:
URL: http://www.tela.bc.ca/hamster/

Lists useful hamster-related resources.

NetVet
URL: http://netvet.wustl.edu/

A complete zoo on the web! Includes veterinary resources, links to other sites, information on pet care and more.

Yahoo!—Science: Zoology: Animals . . .
URL: http://www.yahoo.com/Science/Zoology/Animals_Insects_and_Pets/Rodents/Hamster

This offers a complete set of hamster links as well as information on hamster care.

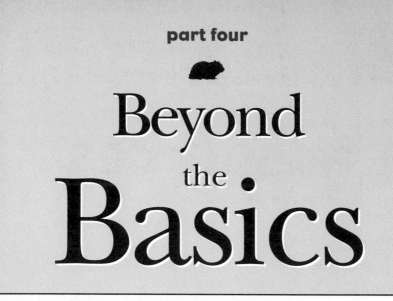

part four

Beyond the Basics

chapter **10**

Resources

Further Reading

Parslow, Percy. *Hamsters.* New Jersey: T.F.H. Publications, Inc., 1995.

Piers, Helen. *Taking Care of Your Hamster: A Young Pet Owner's Guide.* New York: Barron's Educational Series, 1992.

von Frisch, Otto. *Hamsters: A Complete Pet Owner's Manual.* New York: Barron's Educational Series, 1989.

Magazines

Cavy Conservation
6831 Kellog Drive NE
Olympia, WA 98516-9532

A quarterly magazine for owners of small pets (primarily focused on guinea pigs, but covers hamsters and rabbits as well).

Critters USA
P.O. Box 6050
Mission Viejo, CA 92690

An annual magazine for owners of small pets.